2013

WALK TALL

The Hal Leonard Jazz Biography Series

WALK TALL

The Music & Life of Julian "Cannonball" Adderley

CARY GINELL

With a Foreword by Quincy Jones

Hal Leonard Books

An Imprint of Hal Leonard Corporation

Published in 2013 by Hal Leonard Books
An Imprint of Hal Leonard Corporation
7777 West Bluemound Road
Milwaukee, WI 53213

Trade Book Division Editorial Offices
33 Plymouth St., Montclair, NJ 07042

Printed in the United States of America

Book design by Michael Kellner

Ginell, Cary.
 Walk tall : the music and life of Julian Cannonball Adderley / Cary Ginell ; with a foreword by Quincy Jones.
     pages cm. -- (The Hal Leonard jazz biography series)
 Includes bibliographical references, discography, and index.
 ISBN 978-1-4584-1979-8 (pbk.)
 1. Adderley, Cannonball. 2. Jazz musicians--United States--Biography. I. Title.
 ML419.A27G56 2013
 788.7'3165092--dc23
 [B]
                          2012048395

www.halleonardbooks.com

Hipness is not a state of mind, it is a fact of life.

JULIAN "CANNONBALL" ADDERLEY

Contents

Foreword

Quincy Jones

I didn't find Cannonball Adderley. Cannonball found me. It was 1955. I was living in a basement apartment at 55 West Ninety-second Street on the West Side, and one day he and Nat came by. They had just gotten into town from Florida and were looking for a label. Oscar Peterson gave Cannon my number.

I asked him, "Have you ever recorded before?" He said, "Yes," and he gave me this record, a home acetate with a blue label on it. On one side was "Frankie & Johnny," and on the other, I think, an original song or something like that. He pretended he had recorded before, but he hadn't done anything but that one acetate. When I listened to it, that record knocked me on my ass. I remember saying to myself, "Damn, this cat's the next Bird." I had never heard anything like that before. He was groundbreaking, just like Clifford Brown was.

At that time I was working as an arranger and composer and A&R for EmArcy Records and Bobby Shad. Two years later, we made a deal with Philips to sign all of our jazz artists for $100,000 apiece. That was unheard-of back then. I signed Dizzy Gillespie, Art Blakey, Paul Quinichette, and Clark Terry, my idol and guru since I was twelve years old. But that came later. Cannon was the first.

After the Adderleys left, I called Bobby Shad and I said, "Bobby, this is the cat, man. You got to hear this guy. He's the next Charlie Parker." So Bobby said, "I hear you, I hear you. I don't need to hear him. If you think that much about this guy, I believe you. Now here's what you do. Book the studio, get the engineer, get the musicians, and write the arrangements. I'll see you at the studio on Tuesday." We only had a few days to get the session together—not a whole lot of time. So we went with the flow. Together Cannon and I picked the songs and wrote some others. I remember Cannon and I wrote a song called "Fallen Feathers" that was dedicated to Charlie Parker. We got to the Capitol Studios on Forty-fourth Street and Bobby said, "Take 1." That's all he had to do because all the other stuff was done.

We became close friends. Closer than close. After he and his beautiful wife, Olga, moved to Bel Air, I was invited to his house with all of our friends, including Sidney Miller, every Sunday, relaxin' and groovin,' tellin' lies, drinkin' and stinkin'.

Cannon had a mind as sharp as a tack. He had studied with Professor William P. Foster, who was the band director down at Florida A&M. Foster was a brother, but he didn't even want his students to play boogie-woogie. He taught them music theory and how to read. Cannon was an old-school musician. Every musician from the old school had to read music perfectly. And if you came out of Florida A&M, you knew how to read music.

I remember how robust he always was, and what a beautiful, sparkling, original personality he had. He was smart as well as personable, which was a rare combination. You can tell when someone knows who they are and is happy with who they are. That was Cannon. He had that sense of humor, that congeniality, and that charisma, and knew how to reach out to people in the world. Cannon made everything a joy to receive. Nothing was ever a problem for him. Instead, it was a puzzle, because a puzzle you can always solve.

Nadia Boulanger used to tell me, when I was studying with her in Paris, "Quincy, music will never be more or less than what you are as a human being." That's really true. That's where the music comes from. You can have all the technique and knowledge in the world, but if you haven't lived and don't have your own story to tell, you'll have nothing to say musically. Music is a reflection of who the person is, and whatever "it" was, Cannonball had "it."

Excellence is not an act, it's a habit, and Cannonball Adderley made a habit of excellence. I will never forget him, and neither will my daughter Kidada, for he was her godfather. One of our proudest possessions is Cannon's gold flute that he left her, which hangs on the wall behind my bar along with Dizzy's original upright trumpet. As long as I live, Cannon will always be with us, and deep within our hearts.

Preface
Dan Morgenstern

I missed Cannonball's fabled New York debut but did see him not long after, for the first of many happy times. While more than effective on record—and we are fortunate that he was so well represented, as leader and sideman, studio and live, during his splendid but all-too-brief twenty-year run—Julian (which is what I called him) was most fully appreciated when heard and seen in person. That was when the warmth of his sound, voice, and personality was truly realized in three dimensions.

Julian began his professional life as a teacher, and he never lost that aspect of his persona. This was one reason he became such an effective communicator, on bandstand and stage, and, I'm sure, such a successful bandleader. He just loved to connect with people, and to give them some words to go with the music. In that sense, he was truly a jazz messenger.

But it wasn't just his own music that Julian promoted. His special relationship with the record producer Orrin Keepnews, as an unofficial advisor and talent scout, brought about, most significantly, the overdue emergence of Wes Montgomery and, on an entirely different but charming level, his narration of Riverside's *History of Jazz* LP. For another label he produced an album for singer and alto saxophonist Eddie "Cleanhead" Vinson, who he felt had been undeservedly neglected, and he surely did lots of less visible coat pulling on behalf of other musicians.

Inevitably, a prominent jazz musician as articulate as Julian was enlisted by the media as a spokesman, and he did well in that role. When I was with *Down Beat* I managed to involve Julian in a panel discussion that focused on new currents in jazz, feeling that I would need a voice of reason, and though a gig came up after our date had been set, he showed up for as long as he could (most others would just have begged off). And he did indeed provide that voice in what became a free-for-all. (For readers into ancient history, it was published in *Down Beat's* "Music '66" as "Point of Contact.")

A much more enjoyable point of contact occurred when Julian attended one of the annual meetings of the National Endowment of the Arts' Jazz Advisory Panel. The jazz program had been growing slowly but steadily and had reached a point where there was some decent funding at our disposal, but Julian rightly felt that there should be more. I served on that panel longer than anyone, first as an adviser, then as consultant, and thus had the pleasure of working with a large number of musicians, many of them dedicated to the cause. But none was as inspirational as Julian, who in the course of two days of meetings raised the level of consciousness and ambition to new heights. He would have made a fabulously effective politician. On a lower plane, this also provided an opportunity to observe Julian in his Cannonball role—as eater. We had lunch in situ, so to speak, and fixed our own sandwiches from an ample spread. The ones—and more than one, to be sure—that Julian fixed, with all the trimmings, were truly gargantuan, and were dispatched at a tempo fit for the Adderley Quintet at its fastest.

Mention of the Quintet brings his brother, Nat, to mind. The two were, I'm certain, the closest musical brothers in jazz history, artistically and personally. Their togetherness in ensembles was unique, not least because their rhythmic sense seemed to stem from a single heartbeat. Nat carried on the message after Julian's big heart stopped beating much too soon, but not before the creation of a musical legacy, lovingly traced in these pages by Cary Ginell, and very much still with us.

Introduction
Cary Ginell

My fascination with the music of Cannonball Adderley began when I was a boy of thirteen, immersed in the pop and rock broadcast on Los Angeles radio station KHJ, then at the height of its omnivorous "Boss 30" music format. KHJ was known to have played everything and anything, so long as it was popular. The late 1960s was a time when jazz instrumentals crossed over and became best sellers. Through the radio I discovered hits by Ramsey Lewis ("The In Crowd"), Hugh Masekela ("Grazing in the Grass"), and El Chicano ("Viva Tirado"), and many other hit singles. The songs were rhythmic and jazzy, and all had infectious hooks.

Through my older brother, an inveterate and much more advanced jazz fan, I found other artists who played this catchy music, mostly on 45-rpm singles (we couldn't afford to buy very many LPs on a seventy-five-cent a week allowance) with edited performances of what were longer works on LP. As a Beatles fan, I always was drawn to the colorful yellow-and-orange swirl design Capitol Records used on their singles in those days, so when I was thumbing through my brother's album binder of 45s, I came across a record by the Cannonball Adderley Quintet. The name "Cannonball" fascinated me, so I asked him about it and he put the record on his turntable. The record was "Mercy, Mercy, Mercy." I had already developed a love for soul music, which I was probably drawn to by Ramsey Lewis's music, with its unmistakable gospel swing, and also enjoyed the few Ray Charles records we had in the house; so when I put the needle on "Mercy, Mercy, Mercy," I was instantly captivated.

The song was not just jazzy and soulful, but singable; a good melody always grabbed my attention, and my still developing ear for jazz loved the sound.

In time other Adderley singles became favorites: the ripping excitement of "I'm on My Way" and the exotic beat of "Gumba Gumba." I yearned for more and began checking out jazz LPs from the Brand Library in Glendale, devouring the longer versions of some of his songs, such as "Work Song" and "Jive Samba." As a musician myself, I had a better than average ear, and through the cornucopia of styles I was hearing on KHJ, my musical taste rapidly expanded to include soul jazz, the most accessible kind of jazz for general consumption.

I was never aware of the racial element of music. In listening to all different kinds of styles while growing up, the objectivity of radio's audio-only limitations made it unnecessary to distinguish between white and black performers. Even the 45s that we so eagerly craved did not reveal the races of the performers. Along with a national awakening to civil rights in the 1960s, it is likely that this had something to do with jazz's crossing of racial barriers during this period, when radio stations desegregated themselves by playing whatever was selling, and not just music by one particular racial group.

As it turned out, what happened to me was also happening to other youngsters throughout the United States. Through the portal of Top 40 radio, soul jazz indoctrinated many fans, both white and black, into the world of Jimmy Smith, Ramsey Lewis, and Herbie Mann. In time, I learned the lineage of Cannonball Adderley's development: how he started as a neophyte bop musician but changed with the times, eager to embrace different influences and experiment with music of different cultures, always with a youthful and joyous enthusiasm.

Cannonball Adderley changed jazz because, to him, jazz wasn't just an intellectual process—it was fun. The joy and exuberance of Adderley's music was infectious. You can see it in any of his band's performances that stream over YouTube. As opposed to the stoic, introspective, and self-absorbed musicians of bebop, Cannonball Adderley clearly enjoyed everything he played. But watch him when he is not playing. His right hand is in constant motion, fingers snapping and hand waving in a circular motion to the percolating soulful beat. His feet tap a steady rhythm. He smiles often, especially when Nat is playing cornet. When Cannonball has a good time, his audience does as well.

But for me, the best thing about listening to Cannonball Adderley's records was his spoken introductions. At thirteen, I had no idea what jazz was all about, but Cannonball explained all I needed to know. He spoke not in the pedantic manner of a teacher, but as an entertainer. Still, I couldn't help but learn from those humorous and hip intros to his songs. He always identified the songwriter, explained the derivation of the often kooky-sounding song titles, or, if there was no real explanation, merely chuckled about it, such as on "Mini Mama." It didn't surprise me in the slightest when I later learned that Cannonball had started out as a music teacher himself.

What Cannonball Adderley did was make jazz accessible to the average person's ears. Previously, jazz was an in-group genre. You had to get it from the inside out. With Adderley, you didn't have to understand complex chord progressions, modal scales, or arcane musical references. All you had to do was dig the groove.

Cannonball Adderley exploded onto the jazz scene in the early 1960s by making the same impression on audiences as he did on me. He brought an enthusiasm for his music to nightclubs around the world, expanding jazz's boundaries with a fresh exuberance as the music progressed from the bebop of the 1940s and '50s to combine with gospel and soul to help pioneer the subgenres of hard bop and soul jazz in the '60s. Beginning with his single of "African Waltz," Cannonball Adderley pioneered the barrier-breaking influx of pop-oriented singles into Top 40 radio, which continued throughout the decade.

But Cannonball Adderley's influence was much greater than that of a mere popularizer of the constantly changing sound of jazz. Through his series of music clinics and lectures, Adderley explained and demonstrated the history of jazz to youngsters who had no other means of getting to know the music. Like me, they were too young to attend concerts at nightclubs that served alcohol and had limited means of traveling to places where they could hear his music. So Cannonball brought the music to them, conducting sessions in countless high schools, talking about the music in language they could understand, with a good-natured personality that turned him into a veritable Pied Piper of jazz.

Introduction

In the spring of 1975 I was an undergraduate student at UCLA working at the campus radio station when Cannonball Adderley came to deliver one of his seminars. The radio station was situated in the rear of the student union assembly hall and although I was on the air at the time, I would poke my head out into the hall periodically to hear what was going on. The hall was filled to capacity, and I remember seeing Cannonball, all by himself, giving a freewheeling lecture on jazz punctuated by recorded musical demonstrations. I don't remember much about what he said, mainly because my attention was distracted by my on-air duties at the station, but the image of him and the enthusiastic reaction of the students in the massive hall will stay with me always.

Cannonball Adderley died shortly after that, at the all-too-young age of forty-six. By that time jazz had mutated again, and fusion had become its latest incarnation. I have no doubt that had he lived, Cannonball would have absorbed whatever the latest trend was in jazz and would have spearheaded still other avenues it would take in succeeding generations. But Cannonball Adderley embodied the spirit of the 1960s, when everything hip and youthful was the order of the day, and experimentation and joy made learning about jazz an exciting adventure.

My study of Cannonball Adderley's life would not have been possible without the kind assistance of his widow, Olga Adderley Chandler. I knew Olga from her adorable portrayal of Verna Kincaid, sister-in-law of Bill Cosby's character Chet Kincaid in Cosby's first situation comedy. She's still adorable, as is her second husband, the poet and 1960s activist Len Chandler. Through Olga I was able to get in touch with other principals in Cannonball's career, such as Quincy Jones and Roy McCurdy. Olga and Cannonball (she always called him Julian) had a happy marriage, and Olga spoke sweetly and reverently about him. She also provided me with many of the photographs and memorabilia used in the book. Thanks also to Ed Lyon for lending me a long-out-of-print alto saxophone songbook, which helped me understand some of Cannonball Adderley's style and technique. As the publisher of both Adderley brothers, Laurie Goldstein provided valuable insight into other elements of their professional world. At Hal Leonard, John Cerullo eagerly accepted my proposal of Cannonball Adderley as the first in a planned series of biographies of underdocumented jazz greats. Lastly, I would like to thank my wife, Gail, who put up with, and learned to like, many of the Adderley records I played in my office over and over again as I dissected his life, style, and career.

1

CANNIBAL

The annals of jazz are filled with examples of legendary musicians beginning their lives as products of broken homes, divorce, indigent upbringing, and other aspects of life grouped under the clichéd heading of "insurmountable odds." This is not the case with the formative years of Cannonball Adderley, for his family was not only stable and supporting throughout his life, but the chief influence on the kind of man he would become.

The Adderleys first arrived in the United States in 1883 when Daniel Campbell Adderley of Nassau in the Bahamas immigrated to Key West, Florida. Daniel would become Cannonball and Nat Adderley's paternal grandparents. Born in 1860, Daniel Adderley was a tailor by trade. He married Charlotte Spatcher, who was also from Nassau, in 1885 or 1886, and the couple had seven children. Charlotte, who was born in 1862, died sometime between the 1900 and 1910 censuses of unknown causes, but Daniel lived to be ninety-five years old, dying in Dade County in 1955. In 1940, at the age of eighty, he finally became a naturalized citizen of the United States.

Of Daniel and Charlotte's seven children, only three survived past 1900. The oldest, Nathaniel Campbell Adderley, was born in 1886 in Key West. Quinten Jerome Adderley, born in 1902, moved to Charlotte, North Carolina, where he worked for the Boy Scouts as scout executive for Negro scouts during World War II. The youngest child, Julian Carlo Adderley, who would become Cannonball and Nat's father, was born on January 3, 1904. He married Jessie Lee Johnson (familiarly known as "Sugar") in 1928; she gave birth to their oldest son, Julian Edwin Adderley Jr., in Tampa, on September 15, 1928.

Pride in musical achievement as well as education had become a hallmark of the Adderley family by the time Julian Jr. was born. Julian's uncle, Nathaniel Adderley, worked as a tailor like his father, but from 1910 to 1918 he was the director of the marching band at what is now Florida A&M University in Tallahassee. His wife, Nettie, worked as a teacher in one of the first schools for black children in Polk County, Florida. (Nettie died in 1987 at the age of 101.) Today, the Nettie L. and Nathaniel C. Adderl(e)y Memorial Scholarship Fund is awarded to deserving students at Bethune-Cookman College who were graduates of high schools in Lakeland, Florida.

Julian Adderley Sr. was a jazz cornetist and teacher who played in the trumpet sections of groups such as the Eagle Eye Shields Band and the Celery City Serenaders, the latter featuring Duke Ellington's future sideman Cootie Williams. While attending FAMU he became a proud member of the school's Marching 100, which at one time had been directed by his older brother. (There was an eighteen-year difference in their ages.) Julian often glowed with pride when telling stories of how the Marching 100 bested minstrel bands in competitions in the 1920s. Both Julian and Jessie lived long lives; Julian died in 1989 at the age of eighty-five; Jessie in 1987 at the age of eighty-eight.

The grand tradition of FAMU's Marching 100 goes back to 1892, when the school was known as the State Normal and Industrial College for Colored Students. The original band consisted of only sixteen musicians, but today it has not only become the second largest marching band in the country (second only to the Marching Chiefs of Florida State University), but is responsible for thirty innovative marching techniques that have become standard operating procedure for many high school and collegiate marching band programs throughout the country. The band's motto, designed to guide the thoughts and rule the actions and lives of its members, perfectly describes the personal attributes of Cannonball Adderley himself: "Highest quality of character, achievement in academics, attainment in leadership, perfection in musicianship, precision in marching, and dedication to service."

When Julian Jr. was an infant, his family moved to Tallahassee, where his parents had been hired to teach at FAMU (After Julian was born, the 1930 census listed his father's occupation as an orchestra musician, while his mother worked as a clerk in a store.) Julian started listening to jazz on the family radio—the first one in the neighborhood—when he was just a toddler. By the age of three, he had become a fan of remote jazz broadcasts from New York's Cotton Club, the focus of the jazz world during the Harlem Renaissance of the 1920s and '30s. In July 1931 Cab Calloway replaced Duke Ellington as leader of the Cotton Club house band and was riding high on the success of his signature song, "Minnie the Moocher," recorded that March. The midnight broadcasts were aired from coast to coast on the NBC Red network, and Julian would stay up late listening to the exciting sounds. Calloway was the rock star of his day; the most identifiable aspect of his act was the "hi-de-ho" call-and-response he had with the club's patrons. It was one of the earliest examples of a jazz entertainer directly relating to an audience and foreshadowed Adderley's own ability to communicate with his fans in a later era. One night, a tube blew out in the family radio, and Adderley recalled crying inconsolably, utterly mystifying his parents, who had not realized how much their son loved listening to the broadcasts.

On November 21, 1931, the Adderleys added another son to the family, named Nathaniel Carlyle after his uncle. Like his older brother, Nathaniel, who was always called Nat, was also introduced to music at an early age; Nat and his older brother learned how to sing almost before they were able to read.

Julian's first experience seeing a live jazz performance was probably in 1933, when his father took him to the City Auditorium in Tampa to see a concert by Fletcher Henderson and his orchestra. Henderson's big band, which was suffering from the lingering effects of the Great Depression, broke up in 1935, whereupon Henderson went to work as an arranger for Benny Goodman. The Henderson band included the legendary tenor saxophonist Coleman Hawkins. The experience of hearing the Hawk had a pronounced effect on Julian, and he fell in love with the sound of the saxophone.

Julian began taking piano lessons when he was in the second grade, but he disliked his teacher and did not take lessons for long. By the time he was eight, he had already had started a record collection, favoring the bands of Lucky Millinder, Earl Hines, Andy Kirk, and Chick Webb. Recognizing his son's affinity for these groups, Julian's father bought him his first instrument: a trumpet, acquired from the Sears Roebuck catalog. Almost immediately the boy started trying to imitate the sounds he was hearing on the family radio. The Adderley brothers, who were Episcopalian, enjoyed going to the local Tabernacle Baptist Church after Sunday services for a fish fry and to listen to the jumping, swinging sounds of Baptist gospel shouts. This experience laid the groundwork for the often gospel- and blues-flavored songs the Adderleys favored in later years.

Although he liked the big bands of the 1930s, Julian also took notice of the less prominent smaller units, which usually consisted of contingents from larger groups, such as the Benny Goodman Trio and Quartet. But the band that really caught Julian's attention was one led by bassist John Kirby, a group that was specifically created as a small unit. In later years Adderley occasionally played and recorded with large orchestras, but his own groups always consisted of five or six members, with each person playing a significant role.

Julian was different from the other boys in his neighborhood. While his friends wanted to play cops and robbers, all he wanted to do was play jazz. When he was twelve, Julian formed a band with Nat, then nine, and some of their schoolmates that became known as the Royal Swingsters. One friend, a drummer named Lonnie Hayes, started calling Julian "Cannibal" because of his gargantuan appetite. Tampa residents who were unfamiliar with the term ended up pronouncing it "can-i-bol," which eventually became transformed to "Cannonball."

As a boy soprano, Nat received more tips than anyone else in the band, and when the rest of the band got jealous he was forced to leave. Julian followed out of loyalty, but both brothers eventually returned and stayed with the little group for the next four years, with Nat and Julian pooling the money they earned. Even though they were still children, the money Julian and Nat were able to earn from their jobs was enough to help with the family finances.

Julian tried hard to turn Nat into a musician, but Nat wasn't interested in learning to read music like his brother; he thought all you had to do was hear what was happening and play by ear. Julian was the only one in the group with any formal musical education, and he enjoyed showing off his knowledge. When Nat's voice changed, he gave up singing, and Julian taught him how to play trumpet (mainly so as not to disappoint their father) and read music. Julian was having a lot of trouble with the trumpet embouchure anyway, so he was glad to finally be able to give it up. In 1942 he switched to what he really wanted to play: the saxophone. Nat later recalled that although Julian was an excellent trumpet player, he was limited by his lack of range and endurance.

One day at school, Nat's trumpet was stolen. He went to check out another from the band department, but all they had was a cornet. By the time he earned enough money to buy another trumpet, he had discovered that the cornet was easier for him to play. It remained his instrument for the rest of his life.

The alto wasn't the first saxophone that Julian chose to play. He wanted to play tenor, but with World War II on, saxophones of any kind were scarce, so Julian could not afford to be choosy. He purchased a beat-up alto and started playing it in the styles of his favorite tenor players—not only major stars such as Coleman Hawkins and Lester Young, but also lesser-known performers, including Budd Johnson (of the Earl Hines orchestra), Julian Dash and Paul Bascomb (both with Erskine Hawkins), and Buddy Tate (a mainstay in Count Basie's unit). His first idols on the alto were Johnny Hodges, Benny Carter, and Jimmy Dorsey, all players with impressive technical chops.

In addition to playing melodically, Julian favored the gutsy, swinging styles of Young, Hawkins, Ben Webster, Chu Berry, and Don Byas, among others. He eagerly studied the complex ideas coming from a young alto saxophonist in Jay McShann's orchestra, a twenty-two-year-old prodigy from Kansas City named Charlie Parker. Parker later joined a new band led by trumpeter Dizzy Gillespie, who was one of Nat's idols. With the help of a trombonist friend named Jaki Byard, the brothers discovered a whole new world of music, listening intently to the Gillespie band's bebop 78s on a jukebox at a local greasy spoon.

By this time, the fifteen-year-old Julian was itching to go on the road with local jazz bands, but his parents would not let him. He was allowed, however, to play in the band for the famous Rabbit's Foot Minstrels, a long-running minstrel and variety troupe that toured as a tent show in the South between 1900 and 1950.

Always an outstanding student, Julian finished high school in 1943 when he was only fifteen years old and promptly enrolled at Florida A&M University, where his parents taught. When Nat was old enough, he, too attended school there, and in time both brothers joined the college jazz band, which included at one point a talented blind piano player named Ray Robinson, who would later became better known as the soul music icon Ray Charles. In his autobiography, Charles recalled, "They'd be doing the current stuff going 'round, very hip charts of 'Tippin' In' and 'After Hours,' the big Erskine Hawkins hits. I especially loved 'After Hours,' with that nice bluesy piano feel."

It was almost as if Julian had put himself on the fast track to finish school as quickly as he could so he could go out on the road and play jazz. College proved to be no problem for him, and he graduated in 1946, not quite eighteen years old. For the next two years he toured with regional bands and also played stints with Buddy Johnson and Lucky Millinder's orchestras. The big-band era was quickly fading, however, and the giants of jazz were no longer able to sustain large groups. Julian soon found himself having trouble finding gigs. In the fall of 1948, his prospects for steady work were still bleak, so he took a job as band director at Dillard High School in Fort Lauderdale. The Cannonball nickname was forgotten, and he became plain Mr. Julian Adderley again. Other than playing a New Year's Eve gig aboard the *Mon Lei*, the Chinese junk of Robert Ripley, host of *Believe It or Not!*, he didn't touch his saxophone for the entire school year.

After a few years at Dillard, Julian resigned himself to a career as a schoolteacher. Jazz was all but dead in south Florida anyway. He had heard nothing exciting going on in New York, Chicago, or Philadelphia, and now even the vaunted Dizzy Gillespie orchestra had broken up. In 1950 he saw a young Miles Davis perform in a club, but Davis was strung out on heroin at the time, and his performance was unimpressive, to say the least.

In 1951 Julian was drafted into the army, but he had become so uninterested in performing that he didn't even try out for the army band. College graduates in the army were rare, especially African American ones, and it wasn't difficult for Adderley to rise through the ranks quickly; at one point he even considered attending officer candidate school. An alto player from Detroit found out that Julian played sax and convinced him to try out for the Thirty-sixth Army Dance Band in Fort Knox, Kentucky, a group Julian would eventually lead. (The band would include two other future jazz greats: the trombonist Curtis Fuller and the future Adderley Quintet pianist Junior Mance.) The army band gig rekindled Julian's passion for performing ("I got the bug again," he recalled), and he promised himself that he would do everything he could to make it in the music business when he returned to civilian life.

After his discharge in 1953, Julian studied reed instruments at the U.S. Navy School of Music in Washington, D.C., in the process adding clarinet and flute to his musical arsenal. The following year he returned to his teaching job at Dillard, sharpening his skills by backing singers in commercial nightclubs in the evenings and on weekends. He considered himself an average, even second-rate alto player but thought that if he could make it as a member of the Stan Kenton or Woody Herman orchestra his dreams would be fulfilled. Between his teaching job, playing local nightclubs, and selling cars, Julian was earning $10,000 a year, a good salary for African Americans at the time.

Meanwhile, his brother Nat had contracted musician's wanderlust, and in the summer of 1954 he got a job playing on the road with Lionel Hampton's orchestra. Although Julian Sr. encouraged his sons in their musical aspirations, he tried to prevent them from becoming professionals. There were several reasons for this. He often told his sons a story about when he was playing with a band in Tennessee and got stranded, forced to pick beans in a field in order to earn enough money to get back home. After Nat got the job offer from Hampton, his father told him about the life of a musician, not wanting his sons to suffer the indignities he had endured as a professional trumpet player. Eventually, and reluctantly, he allowed Nat to go. But when he visited Nat in New York he was impressed with the professionalism of Hampton's organization.

While in New York, Nat listened to as many musicians as he could, staying out late every night, attending shows at nightclubs on Fifty-second Street and in Greenwich Village. After six months, Nat invited Julian to visit him in New York. It was Christmas, and it was Julian's first trip to the Big Apple. When Hampton found out that Nat's older brother was an alto player, he asked him to sit in with the group. Impressed with Julian's ability, he even offered him a job, but Hampton's wife, Gladys, who was the real force behind the band, vetoed the offer in the belief that having two brothers in the orchestra would result in the formation of cliques. Although Nat was disgusted by Gladys's overbearing decision, he stayed with the band. But his time with them didn't last long. After choosing to attend the birth of his son, Nat Jr., instead of playing a date at the Apollo Theater, Gladys Hampton summarily fired him. He joined a blues band led by Paul "Hucklebuck" Williams in 1955 while also freelancing with other smaller groups.

In March Charlie Parker, the driving force of the bebop movement, died of a heroin overdose at the age of thirty-five, sending the entire New York jazz establishment into mourning. Parker was idolized by not only his fellow musicians and the public, but by jazz critics as well. The jazz intelligentsia sensed a void and was eagerly searching for someone to fill the role of king of the alto saxophone. At that propitious time in history, Nat Adderley invited his brother Julian to join him once again in New York.

2

A NEW YORK MINUTE

The Café Bohemia was one of many small nightclubs in Manhattan that featured regular jazz performances. Located at 15 Barrow Street in Greenwich Village, it was originally opened by a hood named Jimmy Garofalo in 1949 as a strip joint. One day in early 1955 Charlie Parker wandered into the club and sat in with the house band. According to Charles Mingus, Parker owed Garofalo a tab and offered to play for it. Realizing the star power that he had at his hands, Garofalo turned the place into a jazz club; it became a new Village center for bebop. Unfortunately for Garofalo, Parker died before he could ever play there. But word had gotten out about Parker's forthcoming association with the club, and where Bird went, others flocked. A new house band was hired, led by bassist Oscar Pettiford, that also included pianist Horace Silver, drummer Kenny Clarke, trombonist Jimmy Cleveland, and reedman Jerome Richardson.

Julian Adderley came to New York to take some graduate courses at New York University and was actually considering enrolling to get his master's degree. His brother offered to share driving chores on the long trip up from Florida and told Julian about some possible gigs he could play in the evenings, so the alto sax was put in the trunk along with the luggage. The two left town on Friday, June 17, and on Sunday, June 19, Nat and Julian arrived in Manhattan, where they met the trombonist George "Buster" Cooper, a friend of Nat's from the Hampton band. Nat and Buster wanted to drop in to visit their friend Jimmy Cleveland, who was playing with Pettiford's bebop band at Café Bohemia. Julian later recalled that Nat had arranged for Julian to play a gig with an R&B singer (possibly Ruth Brown), so Julian took his sax with him. After picking up Buster's brother, Steve, the four arrived at the club and took seats in the back of the long, narrow room.

The gig hadn't started yet because Jerome Richardson had not arrived, purportedly because he was attending a recording session (though his name doesn't appear on the roster of any recording sessions held that evening). Musicians had an unwritten rule that if someone was scheduled for a recording date, a substitute could fill in at a gig; however, Richardson's sub had not shown up, and it was getting close to showtime. The meticulous Pettiford refused to go on without an alto and desperately looked around the room to see if he could recognize anyone who might be able to fill in.

Cinderella stories in jazz are not unknown, but none are more explosive than what happened that night at Café Bohemia. Like the ingenue who steps in for the star who's broken an ankle, Julian Adderley was exactly the right person in exactly the right place at exactly the right time. Looking around the room, Pettiford spied saxophonist Charlie Rouse in the audience and asked him if he could fill in for Richardson, but Rouse said he didn't have his horn with him. Then Pettiford spied the Adderleys and the Cooper brothers sitting in the back with four instrument cases. (In New York, one never leaves an instrument in an unattended car.) Pettiford took Rouse aside and said, "Man, there's some guy in the back with an alto; you can transpose those tenor parts." Rouse knew Julian from when they had played a date together in Florida, so he went back to say hello; but instead of asking to borrow his horn, he asked Julian to sit in with Pettiford's band. It would be a great gag, Rouse thought—getting Julian Adderley, a music teacher from Florida, a player of lounge music who backed pop and R&B singers, to sit in with one of the great bebop bands in New York City.

Julian never hesitated. "Certainly," he said, and unpacked his alto. Despite his eagerness, Adderley later recalled that he was scared to death at being railroaded into playing with Pettiford's group with no notice and no rehearsals.

Pettiford was miffed that he had to start his gig with an unknown amateur and decided to teach the newcomer a lesson. For his first tune he called off "I Remember April," tapping off a faster tempo than normal just to make an example of Julian. When it came time for his alto solo, Julian played it with gusto and authority, letting loose a flurry of notes that showed that he had intently studied all of Charlie Parker's recorded solos.

The second song was "Bohemia after Dark," a Pettiford composition that contained some sinewy and difficult-to-navigate melodic lines. Once again Julian breathed fire and brimstone, garnering wild applause from the crowd in the smoky club. When the song was over, Pettiford was impressed, and he invited Julian to remain for the rest of the set. After each number the admiration for Julian's powerful playing increased, and the crowd grew more and more excited as they listened to the rotund twenty-six-year-old's inventive solos.

Sometime during the evening a man came up to Nat and asked him who the new alto player was. Thinking the man was a union representative, Nat, thinking quickly, blurted out, "I don't know. I think he comes from Florida and he's called Cannonball." Julian hadn't been called that since he started teaching at Dillard, but the name "Cannonball" was the first thing that came into Nat's head. The man turned out to be Jimmy Garofalo himself, who promptly went up to the bandstand and told the cheering crowd that the mystery alto player who had blown everyone away with his playing was called "Cannonball." From that moment on, Julian Edwin Adderley would become Cannonball (or Cannon) to everyone except his wife, his mother, and his father.

News about Cannonball Adderley's debut at Café Bohemia spread like wildfire. All people could talk about was the alto man who called himself Cannonball and played like Charlie Parker. The jazz alto players Jackie McLean and Phil Woods were in the audience the night Cannonball made his debut; both were astounded at the prowess of this neophyte. The news didn't make it to *Down Beat* magazine until the August 24 issue, after Cannonball had returned to Florida to resume teaching, but by that time Cannonball's reputation had been secured. Under the headline "Unknown Gets Big Jazz Date," the brief story helped perpetuate the comparisons with Charlie Parker: "Described by many musicians who have heard him as 'the greatest since Bird,' a new and completely unknown arrival from Fort Lauderdale, Fla., known simply as Cannonball, was signed last month by EmArcy." The article went on to describe Cannonball's accidental gig, reporting that the young saxophonist had "amazed musicians when he sat in at the Café Bohemia, and was promptly besieged by offers from record companies."

Cannonball had been scheduled to start his classes at NYU the next day, but his college career was waylaid by the beginning of a career in the city. Pettiford offered him a job playing at Café Bohemia, and after taking a day off he played six straight nights at the club. Miles Davis, who was a regular at the club on his nights off, witnessed Cannonball in his New York debut. Davis was scheduled to open at the club with his own group in July and was instantly impressed when he heard the 265-pound Cannonball play the blues, marveling that no one had heard of him. "Even white critics were raving about his playing," Davis recalled in his autobiography. "All the record labels were running after him. Man, he was hot that quick."

After playing with Cannonball for the entire week, drummer Kenny Clarke invited both Julian and Nat to play on his next date for Savoy Records, which Clarke had arranged with Savoy producer Ozzie Cadena. The session took place on June 28, 1955, one week after Cannonball began playing regularly with Pettiford. Two other members of Pettiford's band were recruited to play on the session—pianist Horace Silver and saxophonist Jerome Richardson—but Cadena decided against using Pettiford himself after refusing to agree to Pettiford's demand that Silver be fired. Instead, Clarke hired twenty-year-old bassist Paul Chambers, who had been playing with a trio at the club opposite Pettiford's band. He also added twenty-two-year-old trumpeter Donald Byrd, later to become a major figure in the funk/soul-jazz revolution of the 1960s and '70s. Both Chambers and Byrd were making their recording debuts.

The group recorded six tunes that day at the Rudy Van Gelder studios in Hackensack, New Jersey. The set included the ironically titled "With Apologies to Oscar" (based on the chord changes to "Sweet Georgia Brown") and the aforementioned "Bohemia after Dark," which eventually become a standard crowd-pleaser in Cannonball's own Quintet. Cannonball's penchant for ballads made its first appearance with the standard "Willow Weep for Me," in which he was showcased and accompanied by Silver, Chambers, and Clarke, the three other horns sitting the number out.

The cover of the album, issued as Savoy MG-12017, featured a photograph of the marquee of Café Bohemia (with its noteworthy misspelling "restraurnt"), "the jazz corner of the world," the names of the musicians, and photographs of the band members on the club's bandstand.

Sometime later, probably after Cannonball signed with Mercury, Savoy revised the cover to take advantage of Cannonball's celebrity status. The new photograph featured the musicians surrounding Kenny Clarke and his drum set, with the title "Bohemia after Dark" printed across the top. The shot was casual: Chambers wore a sleeveless tank top, and except for Silver, who wore a striped golf shirt, the rest of the band in was in white shirtsleeves. The only other words on the cover besides the title were "featuring Cannonball," situated prominently in the lower right-hand corner. No mention is made of Clarke or any other musicians—only Cannonball. Adderley's instantaneous fame, rocket-launched by his sensational appearance at Café Bohemia, had superseded that of anyone else in the group, even its leader. A third cover eventually replaced this one, featuring a provocative image of a topless model coyly standing next to an off-kilter lamppost.

The Pettiford gig went for a second week, and then after a July 4 break, the band proceeded to an unspecified club in Manhattan, where they played until July 10. By this time Cannonball was being courted by some of the major labels in town, so Savoy hurriedly scheduled a solo session for him, knowing that he would probably end up signing with one of them. The session was held on July 14, once again at the Van Gelder studios. For this date Cannonball handpicked a quintet with the configuration that he would use for his entire career; it consisted of his brother Nat, Chambers, Clarke, and pianist Hank Jones.

All of the songs on Cannonball's first album under his own name were written by Julian except the standard "Flamingo," showcasing the brothers' love for blues right from the start. Like the Clarke LP, *Presenting Cannonball*, released one week later, featured an album-cover photo of the Quintet members surrounding Clarke's drums. Once again Cannonball's surname was left out; the explosiveness implied by his first name was all that was necessary. Both discs received raves from *Down Beat*'s reviewer, Nat Hentoff.

After the session, Cannonball resumed his gig with Pettiford while he decided on his next move. Miles Davis had become friendly with Cannonball by this time, as well as with Chambers, whom he recruited to join his own band. Davis, by then a longtime veteran of the New York record-label wars, provided the naïve Cannonball with some seasoned advice, recommending that he talk to Alfred Lion at Blue Note Records. Lion was not only trustworthy; he would leave Cannonball alone in the studio and not interfere with his creativity. Davis also recommended that Cannonball engage the services of John Levy, a former bass player with George Shearing who had become a personal manager. Davis told Cannonball that although he admired his technique, he'd have to do something about "some of the silly chords he was playing." According to Davis, "I told him he ought to change the way he approached them—he just kind of fluffed me off."

Despite his meteoric rise, Cannonball remembered his father's advice and was still not sure whether life as a freelance jazz musician would be better than the stable teaching position he had back home in Florida. He spent just one week listening to various offers and then, with the fall academic year in mind, decided to sign with Mercury Records. His albums were to be released on the label's new jazz subsidiary, EmArcy—a decision Cannonball would come to regret.

3

THE NEW BIRD

When Cannonball Adderley signed with Mercury Records, the label was an up-and-coming force in the jazz world. Started in Chicago in 1945 by Irv Green, Mercury made immediate headway through its judicious signings of important pop vocalists, including Frankie Laine, Patti Page, and Vic Damone, as well as such jazz stars as Erroll Garner, Oscar Peterson, and Buddy Rich. In the late 1940s it added masters from the Keynote label to its catalog, putting out works by the jazz notables Lester Young, Coleman Hawkins, and Count Basie. Acquisition of the National label brought seminal recordings by Billy Eckstine's orchestra, a pioneering group at the dawn of the bebop era. The impresarios John Hammond and Norman Granz climbed on board early, although they were gone by the mid-1950s. Bobby Shad, another enterprising jazz fan and producer, took their place. Only in his mid-thirties, Shad had already built an impressive history in the jazz recording world, having worked for Savoy and National producing sessions of jazz (Charlie Parker) as well as R&B and blues (Lightnin' Hopkins). In 1948 he founded the Sittin' In With label, and in 1951 he joined Mercury as director of artists and repertoire (A&R). In 1954 Shad created a spin-off jazz subsidiary of Mercury called EmArcy (a phonetic pronunciation of the acronym for Mercury Record Corporation). By the end of its first year, EmArcy had released albums by the jazz greats Dinah Washington, Art Blakey, and Clifford Brown.

Shad was told of Cannonball's Café Bohemia debut by trumpeter Clark Terry and producer and arranger Quincy Jones. Immediately, without ever having heard him play, Shad signed Cannonball to an exclusive five-year contract (the naïve Cannonball didn't know that the standard agreement was for three years). Jones himself was put in charge of arranging the songs at Cannonball's first session, which took place on July 21, 1955, at Capitol Studios in New York—one week to the day after Cannonball's first Quintet session for Savoy. Cannonball's ascendancy was appropriately mercurial, and Shad embarked on a campaign to publicize Cannonball as "The New Bird." Two other sessions, on July 29 and August 5, were booked to complete ten songs for Cannonball's debut LP on EmArcy, which was titled simply *Julian "Cannonball" Adderley*. The photo on the album cover epitomized Cannonball's ebullient personality: a shot of the musician, apparently convulsed by uproarious laughter, with his saxophone on his lap, the "Cannonball" name in bold, bright fire-engine-red script across the center of the picture.

Joining Cannonball at the sessions were his brother Nat on cornet and an eight-piece all-star ensemble consisting of members of Oscar Pettiford's orchestra: James Cleveland on trombone, Jerome Richardson on tenor sax and flute, Paul Chambers on bass, and Kenny Clarke on drums, augmented by baritone saxophonist Cecil Payne and pianist John Williams. On the second day of the session J. J. Johnson replaced Cleveland on trombone, and on the final day Max Roach replaced Kenny Clarke on drums. Shad designed the album to be a showcase for Cannonball's alto, which dominated the songs, the other musicians playing supporting roles and taking occasional solos.

Quincy Jones wrote tasteful "little big band" arrangements for all of the songs. As would become his habit, Cannonball recorded compositions with hidden meanings, such as Jones's "Fallen Feathers"; a wistful number inspired by Charlie Parker's "Parker's Mood"; Cannonball's Cuban-flavored "Nat's Everglade" (simply titled "Everglade" on the LP, in reference to their Florida upbringing); and "Cannonball," a bubbly reflection of Cannonball's joyous personality. The term "blowing session" was never more appropriate then on an uptempo romp that was later ascribed the name "Hurricane Connie," after the destructive storm that blew through the Eastern seaboard the week after the sessions concluded in early August. Cannonball's fondness for standards resulted in the addition of "The Song Is You," the 1917 tango "Rose Room" (which

Benny Goodman later turned into a swing hit), Cole Porter's "You'd Be So Nice to Come Home To," and a dreamy version of "Purple Shades," a 1952 hit for Joni James.

The session was straight-ahead bebop, with none of the blues or funk material that Cannonball would become known for in later years. He was getting his feet wet playing with New York's finest bop musicians, as well as feeling his way performing his and Nat's own compositions.

The first album for EmArcy did what it was supposed to do: show off the mature sound of a new talent on the jazz scene. No matter how vocal Shad was in heralding Cannonball as "The New Bird," everyone, especially Cannonball himself, knew that Parker could never, would never be replaced. As a marketing tool, however, the sobriquet helped get Cannonball's name out to the public, no matter how distasteful its implications for the young sax player.

In its September 21 issue, *Down Beat* heralded Cannonball's new role as a bandleader with a blurb capitalizing on his novel nickname by proclaiming him a "big shot" with EmArcy while also announcing the release of his two sessions for Savoy (his premiere effort with Kenny Clarke, and Cannonball's own debut as a featured artist). After the success of the first few EmArcy albums, Savoy changed the cover of Cannonball's debut album from the group shot to the image of three cannonballs stacked into a pyramid.

A second session, held shortly after the first, was marketed with Nat's name. (The date of the session, listed as September 6, is most likely incorrect: by that time Cannonball had returned to Florida to begin teaching the fall semester at Dillard. It is believed the session most likely took place between August 6 and August 15.) *Introducing Nat Adderley* was released as the first issue in the jazz series of Mercury's new subsidiary label, Wing Records.

This album was marked by two major developments in the career of Cannonball and Nat Adderley. First is the appearance of the Adderleys in their standard quintet configuration (alto sax, cornet, piano, bass, and drums). With the exception of the addition of Yusef Lateef, who joined for a brief period in the early 1960s, and of electronic keyboards beginning in the late '60s, this was the basic instrumentation that Cannonball Adderley would favor for the rest of his career.

The other important element of the album is the array of original songs written by the Adderley brothers. Excepting the Paul Weston–Axel Stordahl standard "I Should Care," all the songs were credited to both Julian and Nat Adderley. Joining them on the session were Horace Silver, winner of a *Down Beat* New Star award and a promising artist in his own right; drummer Roy Haynes (who had worked extensively with Charlie Parker); and bassist Paul Chambers.

Although Nat was the featured player, Cannonball got plenty of time to blow as well, and many of the songs featured contrapuntal conversations between the two. It was an impressive debut for Nat, who showed a definite affinity for the style of Miles Davis. Once again the song titles hinted at elements from the Adderleys' life, including "Fort Lauderdale" (Cannonball's teaching job was still waiting for him), "Two Brothers," and "Little Joanie Walks," inspired by Bob Shad's infant daughter (the original liner notes misidentified her as Shad's niece), who had just taken her first steps.

After completing the session, the Adderleys got back in their car and returned to Florida. Along the way they stopped for a weeklong gig at the Blue Note club in Philadelphia, where they were joined by a local trio consisting of Jimmy "Hen Gates" Foreman on piano, either Jimmy Mobley or Jimmy Rowser on bass, and Specs Wright on drums. Despite the whirlwind success of the past few weeks, Cannonball had no illusions about what he needed to do. He still considered teaching to be the best financial option for him. Because of the gigs and the recording sessions, he had blown his opportunity to take the graduate courses he had intended on taking at NYU, but he knew that he had a teaching job to return to, and the fall semester was about to begin.

For the remainder of 1955 Cannonball taught school during the daytime; at night he assembled a band that played six nights a week at Porky's, a local Fort Lauderdale nightclub. The Porky's gig lasted from September 27, 1955, until the end of January 1956; the only break came when Bob Shad flew Cannonball to New York to participate in Sarah Vaughan's inaugural session for EmArcy (*Sarah Vaughan in the Land of Hi-Fi*), playing in an orchestra led by Ernie Wilkins.

But Shad didn't bring Cannonball all the way up to New York just to be a sideman at someone else's session. In promoting "The New Bird,"

Shad decided to showcase Cannonball fronting a string orchestra led by Richard Hayman, blatantly stealing an idea that had been successfully pioneered by Charlie Parker in 1949. Since then, a number of other jazz artists had utilized this formula, and so, Shad thought, why not try it with Cannonball? The previous week he had scheduled a "jazz plus strings" session for vibraphonist Terry Gibbs, but Gibbs talked him into allowing Manny Albam to craft arrangements for five saxophonists instead. (The resulting effort, titled *Vibes on Velvet*, became a big seller for Gibbs.) No such objection was raised by Cannonball, and the album (*Julian "Cannonball" Adderley and Strings*) was completed as planned, with Cannonball recording a dozen standards on consecutive days in late October.

At the end of the year, Cannonball's contract at Dillard expired, and after some serious thought and discussions with Nat he decided to give playing jazz professionally a try. He later told *Down Beat*:

> I could have worked with somebody else, gone back to New York and taken my chances freelancing, but by this time I was making ten grand a year in Florida. I had this teaching at five grand and I was making $150 a week playing at night, plus I had a couple of side hustles. I sold automobiles—and I did quite well, too; I had that gift of gab. Old ladies, I could sell them any kind of car. It was hard to turn my back on all that and come to New York with nothing. So we decided to organize this band.

The first Cannonball Adderley Quintet included Cannonball on alto sax and Nat on cornet, along with three members of Miami's Local 690 of the American Federation of Musicians: Ray Bryant on piano, Bob Fisher on bass, and Norman McBurney on drums. The group rehearsed for two and a half weeks, then hired John Levy to be their manager.

Levy booked them immediately on a three-city tour on their way to New York, including a week at Storyville in Boston, two weeks at the Blue Note in Philadelphia (with John Coltrane and Red Garland in attendance), and a week at the Las Vegas nightclub in Baltimore. But Cannonball soon realized that a good Florida band didn't necessarily translate into challenging top-flight New York City musicians. Before leaving Florida, Bryant was replaced by Junior Mance, but there was still something seriously wrong with the band's rhythm section. Cannonball later told *Down Beat*:

By the second day in Philadelphia, John Levy decided to fire everyone. Jack Fields, an ex-musician and then owner of the Blue Note, was also somewhat upset. I had gotten great response in that room on the way to Florida with Kenny Clarke, bassist Jimmy Mobley, and pianist Hen Gates, but on the way back, I found out that you can't fool anybody in Philadelphia. Jack lent me some money and I hired Specs Wright as drummer, but I had to keep the bass player a while or give him two weeks' pay. He couldn't keep an even tempo on fast numbers, so we had to stop playing fast things for a while.

By the time the band got to New York in March, the rhythm section had been revamped again. Fisher and McBurney were fired after the first set in Philadelphia, but Cannonball and Nat persuaded Levy not to let Mance go, since he had only just joined. They were replaced by bassist Sam Jones (a friend of the Adderleys from Florida) and drummer Jimmy Cobb. The new Quintet played six nights at Birdland and then went back out on the road, heading first to a two-week gig at Cleveland's Cotton Club and then to four weeks at the Bee Hive Lounge in Chicago.

Sam Jones converted from guitar to bass after hearing records by Oscar Pettiford while playing in his high school dance band. Although Jones gave credit to Jimmy Blanton as being chiefly responsible for elevating the bass from a two-beat instrument to the backbone of a band, he names Ray Brown as the musician who really took the bass to another level. He also admired the work of Scott LaFaro, an influential bass player of the 1950s who died at the age of twenty-five in a tragic automobile accident.

On April 24 the Quintet returned to New York for a recording session for EmArcy, only to learn that instead of playing their own session, Cannonball and Junior Mance, and not the others were being asked to back singer Dinah Washington on another "with strings" album. It would be a year before Shad would record the Adderley Quintet itself, an elapse of time that led Cannonball to regret his hasty signing.

Shad's reluctance to showcase the Quintet most likely disrupted

Cannonball's momentum as a new force in the jazz world and was probably the chief reason the Quintet did not fare well in 1956 and 1957. Another factor was the equally explosive debut of another, more pervasive force in the music world: the epochal signing of Elvis Presley to RCA Victor. After making his debut with the Memphis-based Sun label in 1954, Presley had become a regional phenomenon in the South; but his signing impacted the American music scene like an H-bomb, overwhelming the relatively puny cannonball that had hit the jazz world.

During his first few months as a bandleader, Cannonball had shown signs of establishing his own identity as he stubbornly fought Shad's "New Bird" appellation. On May 24 the Quintet began a two-week gig at New York's Basin Street East, a swanky nightclub located in the Shelton Towers Hotel on Lexington Avenue. *Down Beat*'s eminent jazz critic Nat Hentoff was impressed by the changes he perceived in Cannonball's style. Hentoff noted Cannonball's obvious talent and technical ability when he first saw the saxophonist at Café Bohemia but thought his playing "lacked cohesion," feeling that he often substituted a "machine-gun run of notes" for logical construction in his solos. Hentoff also was turned off by what he perceived as Cannonball's sometime acrid tone. But upon Cannonball's return to New York, Hentoff noted Cannonball's rounder tone and "more exciting musical architecture." Although still strongly under the influence of Charlie Parker, Cannonball was quickly developing his own voice. "The man has tremendous command of his horn," remarked pianist George Shearing, for whom John Levy had played bass. (Levy was now Shearing's manager as well as the Adderleys'.)

Hentoff also applauded the work of Nat Adderley, saying that the cornetist played "with individual imagination, heart, firstrate [*sic*] time, and . . . steadily maturing structural skill." The rhythm section of Junior Mance, Sam Jones, and Specs Wright was also an improvement; Hentoff approved of their ability to "swing from the floor."

The Quintet's set was dominated by the Adderleys' original compositions, whose melodies, Hentoff noted, though conducive to free-flowing solos, were not particularly memorable. More important, however, Hentoff made mention of the ebullient, astute personality Cannonball was displaying on the stage for the first time, calling him "Churchillian" and one of the best rhetoricians on the jazz club circuit.

"Cannonball never forgets to identify the numbers and the players. Therefore, unlike those many jazz leaders who fail to announce their sets, Cannonball has an audience rapport going for him from in front." Hentoff concluded with a ringing endorsement: "This is a combo both to watch and to enjoy now."

Yet, at the time the Hentoff review appeared, Cannonball and Nat were recording as the "Cannonball Adderley Orchestra," cells in a ten-piece "midi-band" (somewhere between a big band and a combo in size) performing arrangements by Ernie Wilkins on an album that would become *Cannonball Adderley in the Land of Hi-Fi*. The album only featured one Adderley original ("Blues for Bohemia"); one song, however—Tommy Turrentine's "T's Tune"—signaled a new style that would later be called "soul jazz." Inexplicably, the LP wouldn't be released until the following year, yet again spoiling Cannonball's musical momentum on the jazz scene.

In July 1956, while spending three weeks at Basin Street East, the Cannonball Adderley Quintet finally had its first recording session, with Al McKibbon replacing Sam Jones on bass. But despite rave reviews for their live performances from even the most hard-bitten jazz critics, EmArcy did not get an album by the Quintet out on the market until well into 1957. The July 1956 sessions languished in the vaults for over a year, and when they were finally issued, they were under Nat's name and not Cannonball's. Gil Fuller provided the arrangements, which included a number Cannonball had written that he had introduced at Basin Street East as "Sermonette for Cornet," shortened to "Sermonette" for the LP. Nat wrote "Hopping John" in honor of John Levy, and "Hayseed" was the result of Nat's combining the standards "Cocktails for Two" and "It's a Lovely Day Today." "Room 251," composed by the Adderleys' old friend Jaki Byard, referred to the Adderleys' hangout at the Alvin Hotel on Fifty-second Street opposite Birdland, a popular gathering spot for such musicians as Lester Young.

On October 21 the Quintet made its first appearance on television in an episode of NBC's *Monitor* program, which was broadcast the following month. The remainder of the year was spent playing dates at the Marina and the Spotlite Room in Washington, D.C., and the Blue Note clubs in Chicago and Philadelphia. (The *Monitor* program was recorded at the

Chicago date.) In late November they made their first trip to the West Coast, where they appeared at the Blackhawk in San Francisco and Jazz City in Los Angeles. While in L.A., Cannonball backed vocalist Sylvia Sims on the *Stars of Jazz* program on KNBC-TV. But with all this activity, and with their reputation spreading throughout the jazz world, there was a disquieting silence from EmArcy, which did not find it important to capitalize on the Cannonball Adderley Quintet's increasing popularity.

In January 1957 Cannonball moonlighted as "Ronnie Peters," the first of several pseudonyms he used to record under during his contract with EmArcy. The album, titled *Plenty, Plenty Soul*, was made for Atlantic Records and featured a group assembled by Milt Jackson, the Modern Jazz Quartet's vibraphonist. The session was produced by Nesuhi Ertegun and featured arrangements by Cannonball's friend Quincy Jones, who conducted an all-star orchestra including trumpeter Joe Newman, drummer Art Blakey, and three old friends from the Café Bohemia days: Jimmy Cleveland, Horace Silver, and Oscar Pettiford. Seven tunes were recorded, with Cannonball featured on the three titles that appeared on the LP's side 1: the title track, Quincy Jones's "Boogity Boogity," and Jackson's "Heartstrings." The word "soul" was now being officially bandied about in jazz. In the liner notes, Jackson defined the term as "what comes from within; it's what happens when the inner part of you comes out. In my case, I believe that what I heard and felt in the music of my church was the most powerful influence on my musical career." The song "Plenty, Plenty Soul" is a twelve-bar blues co-composed by Jackson and Quincy Jones and features a decidedly un-Birdlike solo by Cannonball.

"Sermonette" was included on side 2 of the album, but, ironically, Cannonball was not present at that session, which featured tenor man Lucky Thompson as the sole saxophonist. The contributions of "Ronnie Peters" failed to get a mention in Nat Hentoff's liner notes.

Frustrated with EmArcy's lack of attention to his career, Cannonball guest-starred on a February session led by trumpeter Louis Smith, who was making his debut as a bandleader for the short-lived Transition label. Transition went out of business before the album could be released, but it was picked up and issued by Blue Note under the title *Here Comes Louis Smith*.

Smith's background was remarkably similar to Cannonball's; he had earned a music degree at the University of Michigan and taught music at Booker T. Washington High School in Atlanta while jamming in clubs at night. In addition to Cannonball, Smith's Quintet also included pianist Duke Jordan, bassist Doug Watkins, and drummer Art Taylor. Recalling the session in 1998, Smith told Chris Sheridan: "I had played in band battles against Cannonball when we were both at university in the 1940s, but Doug Watkins didn't know either of us. He thought that would make it an easy date, so he didn't take his topcoat and cap [off] to play. Cannon soon had him working hard, and by the time we finished, he was down to his vest and trousers."

For this session, Cannonball called himself "Buckshot La Funke." The annotator Leonard Feather went along with the gag, writing, "Buckshot La Funke (of the Florida La Funkes) is one of the modern alto giants, described by Nat Adderley as 'my favorite soloist.'"

Two days after recording as "Buckshot La Funke," Cannonball was back in the EmArcy studios for a three-day session with his Quintet. Sam Jones had returned to play bass, and the Adderleys were finally looking forward to getting some much-needed publicity from EmArcy. But of the seventeen titles recorded, only nine were released that year (on the EmArcy LP *Sophisticated Swing*). The remaining sides were held back for four years, emerging only to capitalize on Cannonball's subsequent success with Riverside on the Mercury LP *Cannonball Enroute*.

Only one Adderley original, Nat's exciting "Another Kind of Soul," appeared on *Sophisticated Swing*, but this did not detract from the further refining of the Quintet's sound. Five of the songs were contributed by bass players: two by the Quintet's Sam Jones and three by the Adderleys' close friend Gene Wright, who at the time was a member of the Dave Brubeck Quartet. The others included Cannonball's lush treatment of two standards (Victor Young's "Stella by Starlight" and Rodgers and Hart's "Spring Is Here") and a version of the pianist Duke Pearson's "Tribute to Brownie," a tribute to the late trumpeter Clifford Brown.

For the first two weeks of March 1957 the Quintet embarked on a tour of southern colleges; they then took the rest of the month off before returning to New York for a stint at Birdland. There were many other open dates in 1957: the Quintet was finding it hard to gain any traction, and the group was experiencing financial stress over the debt they were incurring from their days spent on the road with little or no support from their label.

On July 5 they got a major publicity boost when they made their first appearance at the vaunted Newport Jazz Festival in Newport, Rhode Island. The previous summer Newport had become the most prestigious live event in the jazz world , thanks to an electrifying performance by the Duke Ellington Orchestra highlighted by saxophonist Paul Gonsalves's supercharged twenty-seven-chorus tenor solo on a medley of "Diminuendo in Blue" and "Crescendo in Blue." In 1957 the festival was doubled to encompass four days, and Cannonball found himself performing in the same venue as the giants of jazz: Ella Fitzgerald, Billie Holiday, Count Basie, Coleman Hawkins, Gerry Mulligan, Roy Eldridge, Lester Young, and dozens more.

Cannonball's Quintet played a half-hour set that afternoon, leading off with Denzil Best's blues "Wee Dot." After concluding the song, Cannonball stepped to the microphone to address the crowd as Professor Adderley: "That, of course, was a blues, which we like to play very much. You'll find it obvious in our performance here this afternoon, because we feel that the blues reflects what jazz should be made of."

The group then continued with a groove-induced version of the Gershwin standard "A Foggy Day" (their studio version, cut in February, still had not been released), followed by a soulful shuffle treatment of "Sermonette" and Sam Jones's "Sam's Tune" and concluding with the exuberant "Hurricane Connie," which thrilled the crowd with its quicksilver chord changes.

A few hours later George Shearing took the stage with his Quintet for his evening performance. During his set, Shearing called Cannonball and Nat up onto the stage, and they joined his Quintet (Toots Thielemans on guitar, Al McKibbon on bass, Percy Brice on drums, and Armando Perazza on congas) in an impromptu performance of "Soul Station," a song that smacked of the blues-soaked feel Horace Silver and others would later concoct. The Adderleys were right in their element and swung along with verve, prompting Shearing to exhale in excitement after it was over: "You don't mind us enjoying ourselves for one night, do you? Whew!"

As exciting as the Newport set was, it was the last gasp of the first incarnation of the Cannonball Adderley Quintet. In May 1960 Cannonball told the *Jazz Review* that "by September of 1957, although we had been working steadily, we were about nine thousand dollars in debt. We had no royalties from our recordings and had only made scale for making them. Besides, a lot of recording costs were charged against us which shouldn't have been."

Cannonball's business naïveté had worked against his immense talents as an innovative and exciting performer. The band had been earning about $1,000 a week, but that was before subtracting 15 percent for Levy and his staff, along with union taxes, withholding taxes, and money taken out for Social Security. With no advances coming in from EmArcy and with few recordings of their own to hang their hats on, Cannonball and Nat found themselves drowning in debt. They began spending money that should have been put away for taxes on gasoline bills, hotel bills, and food. Despite twenty months on the road, they had not increased their earnings at all. In 1957 jazz was losing its young audience to R&B and rock and roll, and only a few jazz acts were doing well, among them Dave Brubeck, Miles Davis, and Chico Hamilton. Cannonball knew that something had to give, and he carefully pondered his next career move.

4

MILESTONE

In the September 5, 1957, issue of *Down Beat,* the writer Don Gold formally introduced Cannonball Adderley to its jazz readers with a full-page profile. After a brief biographical section describing his meteoric rise to fame, Gold proclaimed Cannonball "one of the most personable artists in jazz" and complimented him on his modesty as an artist, his congeniality as a performer, and his gracious personality and relationship with the press. The rest of the article included Cannonball's opinions on a curious palette of random topics, from the political climate in South Africa ("That's the only situation I can think of that's more ridiculous than the southern U.S.") to jelly donuts ("I don't particularly care for them. Give me the old-fashioned donut with the hole in the middle").

The article barely touched on Cannonball's musical philosophy, but buried within it was a telling opinion on singer Mahalia Jackson: "Too much, that's all. Combined with Ray Charles, that kind of singing is the size of soul." The soulful aspect of Cannonball's saxophone solos was not yet fully developed, but this element was not lost on Miles Davis. Dizzy Gillespie invited Cannonball to join his orchestra, and when Miles Davis found out he was hurt and asked Cannonball why he didn't join his band instead. Cannonball's answer was that Davis had never asked him. The Adderley Quintet's financial liabilities were causing its headliner much concern by this time, and he knew that if things didn't change soon, the group would fall deeper and deeper into debt. Despite winning over such hard-boiled critics as Nat Hentoff and Leonard

Feather, the group was still not making enough money to support its musicians.

Cannonball and Miles Davis had a mutually respectful relationship. Davis had long since kicked his heroin habit, cleaned up his act, and signed a recording contract with Columbia Records. Ever since he met Cannonball during his breakout guest gig at Café Bohemia, Davis had been impressed not just with Cannonball's virtuosity, but with his feeling for blues and what was beginning to be called soul—the influence of the church and gospel music on his playing. Although Cannonball had taken Davis's advice and hired John Levy as his manager, he regretted not listening to him regarding his choice of record labels. Nor had he listened to Davis's instructions about utilizing chords in his playing. Cannonball played the right chord changes in his performances, but Davis told him that there were alternative chords he could use to achieve a different sound, something that he began to realize when he started listening to saxophonists such as Sonny Rollins.

In the summer of 1957 Davis began actively recruiting Cannonball to join his group, offering him a salary of $200 more per week than Cannonball and Nat earned jointly at that time. Although Gillespie was a more commercial performer, Davis's offer was attractive, and Cannonball felt that he could learn more by going with Davis. He was ready to join Miles right then and there, but he had to wait until October so he could honor his existing engagements. While waiting for Cannonball to become available, Davis hired the Belgian tenor saxophonist Bobby Jaspar—a good musician, but not what Davis had in mind.

Nat Adderley thought his brother's decision to break up their Quintet was a sound one and didn't hold it against him—he knew that Davis's offer was a good one. After the group broke up, Nat went to work for the trombonist J. J. Johnson.

Davis's group included himself on trumpet, Bobby Jasper on tenor sax, Tommy Flanagan on piano, Paul Chambers on bass, and Philly Joe Jones on drums. Cannonball's first gig with Davis was on October 11, 1957, during their cross-country Jazz for Moderns tour at, ironically, New York's Café Bohemia. The Jazz for Moderns tour was an annual package, with the critic Leonard Feather serving as emcee. Headlining was the George

Shearing Quintet, joined by the Quintets of Gerry Mulligan and Chico Hamilton and the Australian Jazz Quintet.

Davis felt that Cannonball's extroverted, exuberant style balanced his own reserved, moody playing, and the group jelled quickly. The Jazz for Moderns concert series continued with performances at the Keil Opera House in St. Louis on November 12 and Orchestra Hall in Chicago on November 15; it concluded at Carnegie Hall in New York on November 22. After that Davis broke up the group temporarily in order to honor a solo commitment in Paris, where he played on the soundtrack for the Louis Malle film *Ascenseur pour l'échafaud* (Elevator to the Scaffold). While Davis was in Paris, Cannonball played two dates with Dizzy Gillespie and attended a three-day recording session with an Afro-Cuban jazz orchestra led by Machito (Frank Grillo). He rejoined the Miles Davis Sextet on Christmas Eve, beginning a weeklong engagement at the Sutherland Hotel and Lounge in Chicago.

But major changes were coming to the Miles Davis Quintet—changes that would have a pronounced effect not just on Cannonball Adderley, but on the jazz world itself. The first came just after Christmas, when the well-regarded blues-influenced pianist Red Garland replaced Tommy Flanagan. On New Year's Day Davis added tenor saxophonist John Coltrane to his band, making it a sextet. Coltrane had played with Davis before; he originally joined him in 1955, participating in two marathon recording sessions that produced four LPs issued on Prestige Records. But Coltrane's unreliability, fueled by his addiction to heroin, resulted in Davis's firing him and breaking up the group. Several months later he kicked his habit cold turkey and joined Thelonious Monk's Quartet for the last half of 1957, after which Davis rehired him. It was during this period that Coltrane blossomed as a musician, and he was only too glad to reunite with the forward-thinking Davis. Coltrane was a student of Davis's theories about chord structure, and Cannonball would learn much from both of them during his time with Davis's Sextet.

Cannonball later said that no one knew more about chords than John Coltrane. "John knows exactly what he's doing," he wrote in an article about his musical development. "He's gone into the melodic aspects of chords. He may go 'out of the chord,' so-called, but not out of the pattern he's got in his mind."

As a musician, Miles Davis was a master of understatement, a reflection of his introverted personality. By playing with Davis, the outgoing Cannonball came to understand the value of playing less rather than more, especially on ballads. He also learned how to adapt new material to the sound of the band without changing his style. When it was necessary to do so, however, Cannonball recognized the subtleties Davis put into those differences.

When Davis began collaborating with the arranger Gil Evans, he decided to expand his group from a quintet to a sextet by having two saxophones play off of each other. His ideas for reinventing bebop dovetailed perfectly with Evans's sophisticated arranging skills. Davis's idea was to turn bebop upside down: whereas its co-creators, Dizzy Gillespie and Charlie Parker, thought in terms of lots of notes in the higher registers of their respective instruments, Davis wanted to hear fewer notes, played in the middle and lower registers. He also wanted to emphasize modal patterns, which are based on only the white keys of a piano, rather than the traditional Western scale system. To this he wanted to add Cannonball's affinity for blues and sacred music, which he felt would work well in juxtaposition with Coltrane's harmonic chord playing and free-form approach.

When Cannonball first heard Coltrane play blues, he was astonished—not just at his virtuosity, but because Coltrane was the first person he knew who was able to play the blues in a completely different way. The teacher became the student. Although Cannonball soaked up what Coltrane was doing like a sponge, he didn't copy him; combined with Coltrane's explanations of what he was doing, Cannonball's musical knowledge enabled him to adapt Coltrane's ideas to his own playing.

Cannonball's jovial personality also meshed well with the Sextet. In his autobiography Davis recalled that Cannonball was always laughing; Davis admired Cannonball's gentlemanly manner, his intelligence, and his ability to get along with the other band members.

The new group worked on their sound during a two-week engagement at Birdland beginning on January 2, 1958, the day after Coltrane joined. After an additional week at the Continental in Brooklyn, they were ready for a recording session, which began at Columbia's Thirtieth Street studios on February 4 and ended exactly a month later. The sessions resulted in the LP *Milestones*, which became the first in a series of classics the Davis

Sextet recorded over the next two years. The songs were retreads of older songs Davis had recorded but showcased different shadings of the new sound Cannonball was cultivating in partnership with John Coltrane.

Most of the six songs on the album took advantage of Cannonball's affinity for the blues. The title track (listed as "Miles" on the original LP) was the first song Davis wrote using a modal harmonic foundation, with Garland, Chambers, and Jones providing a swinging foundation to Davis's statement of the simple theme. The number featured one of Cannonball Adderley's most memorable and melodic solos with the group. "Two Bass Hit," written by the Modern Jazz Quartet's John Lewis, showcased the opposing personalities of the Sextet's two saxophonists, as the introspective Coltrane played off the extroverted Adderley. The traditional American folk song "Billy Boy" was a surprise choice that featured Red Garland, who had begun emulating the style of Ahmad Jamal, and a dynamic bowed bass solo by Chambers.

On the second day of the session the group recorded the supercharged "Dr. Jekyll" (aka "Dr. Jackle," the nickname of the song's composer, Jackie McLean), during which Coltrane and Cannonball traded furious choruses, utilizing what Ira Gitler would call "sheets of sound" in describing Coltrane's new, vertically constructed chordal style, played in a fluid, sweeping manner so fast that one could barely discern individual notes and was forced to focus instead on their cumulative impact.

The last song, "Sid's Ahead," was a reworking of "Weirdo," which Davis had recorded for Blue Note in 1954. On this track, Davis himself played piano after Red Garland walked out on the session, fed up with Davis, who had told him what to play one too many times.

The *Milestones* sessions were a revelation for Cannonball, who now had new hope for his career after floundering with his own band for the previous two years. With a promising future ahead of him with the Miles Davis Sextet, he was finally looking forward to not only continued musical growth, but also financial stability. His tenure with Miles, however, was never meant to be anything more than temporary, a respite that would enable him to reconstitute his bank account. What he hadn't counted on was the valuable musical education he was getting playing with the group.

There were, however, obligations to his old label that he needed to complete, and so after the March 4 session was concluded, Cannonball went immediately to the Bell Sound Studios for the first of a two-day session with his own group for EmArcy. The sessions produced the album *Sharpshooters*, another exciting collection for the Adderley Quintet, although it would be their last; the group officially disbanded shortly after completing the album. *Sharpshooters* featured two Tadd Dameron compositions: a thrilling version of "Our Delight" and the rambunctious "Stay On It," the latter featuring Cannonball whimsically quoting "Doin' What Comes Naturally," from *Annie Get Your Gun*. Standards always gave Cannonball the opportunity to flex his melodic chops, and he played gorgeous solos on Johnny Burke and Bob Haggart's "What's New" and the show tune "If I Love Again," from an obscure 1933 stage musical called *Hold Your Horses*. The most interesting track was Thelonious Monk's "Straight, No Chaser," taken at a bluesier, more leisurely tempo than the warp-speed version recorded with Miles Davis the previous month.

The first Cannonball Adderley Quintet thus passed into history, victimized by a label that still had not issued any of the group's recordings at the time it broke up. Cannonball's subsequent success with Miles Davis saw Mercury eventually capitalize on his fame by releasing its backlog of recordings made since 1956. But by then, it was too late. Cannonball was now a sideman and would not lead a group of his own again for another two years.

5

CANNONBALL ON A ROLL

Three days after his last session with his Quintet, Cannonball Adderley struck a deal to record for the Blue Note record label. Music historians consider the resulting album, titled *Somethin' Else*, one of the greatest jazz sessions ever recorded: A. B. Spellman, of the National Endowment for the Arts, called *Somethin' Else* a "near perfect" album, a record with "not a wrong note nor throwaway song in its grooves." By now Adderley's working relationship with Miles Davis had become so close that Cannonball was able to convince Davis to play as a sideman, something Davis rarely did. (Blue Note's logs listed the group as Cannonball Adderley's Five Stars.) Why Davis did not insist on top billing as well as creative control at this lofty stage in his career is uncertain, but it's possible that the reason had something to do with the agreement between Davis and Cannonball as well as the mutual admiration the two had for each other.

Cannonball had been floundering because of his desultory relationship with EmArcy, and after three years he was still basically unknown outside the New York jazz community. Davis had a good relationship with the head of Blue Note, Alfred Lion, and may have had some influence in Blue Note's decision to sign Cannonball to play this date. In his 1989 autobiography Davis dealt with the album in two very brief sentences, calling it "very nice" and saying that he did it as a favor to Cannonball. In addition to Davis, Cannonball used Hank Jones on piano, Sam Jones on bass, and Art Blakey on drums. Despite being billed second on the album, Miles Davis played a prominent role on the record, his trumpet dominating many of the songs.

The title track is a musical conversation between Davis and Cannonball. To an irresistible medium-tempo bluesy groove, the two horns play off each other beautifully, with Cannonball providing a restrained counterpart to Davis's trumpet. The standard "Autumn Leaves" started off with a dark-tinged riff on the bass, followed by Davis playing the breezy melody with his signature muted horn while Blakey brushed his snare underneath. Cannonball took his turn at the bridge, delivering a stunningly beautiful solo that ranks with the best in his career. The song ended as it began, with the sinister-sounding bass riff and an ethereal, almost unsettling conclusion by Davis. (Adderley would use a modified version of this arrangement with his own Sextet in the early 1960s.)

Hank Jones provided a cocktail-piano intro to Cole Porter's "Love for Sale," with Davis leading off with the melody. Again, Cannonball took the first chorus as the bass and drums kept things swinging. Davis restated the melody over a subdued rhythm section, with Hank Jones providing a neat bookend to his opening statement.

Nat Adderley's tribute to the Chicago disc jockey Holmes "Daddy-O" Daylie, "One for Daddy-O," is a snakelike blues with a sly bass beat that Cannonball dances around playfully during his solo. Blakey's sinuous, metronomic drumming kept the momentum going through the choruses that followed by Cannonball, Davis, and Hank Jones. (On the reissue CD Davis can be heard asking Lion sardonically, "Is that what you wanted, Alfred?" after the last note fades away.)

A final number from the session, titled "Alison's Uncle" (referring to Cannonball's status after the birth of Nat's daughter that evening), was not included on the original LP, possibly on account of its sprightly nature, which didn't fit the hip, basement-jazz aura of the rest of the tunes. The song was eventually released in Japan twenty years later. Alternatively known as "Bangoon," the song featured the album's only drum solo by Blakey (who hummed along as he played).

After *Somethin' Else*, Miles Davis was getting ready to record another album with his Sextet, but Cannonball was now becoming a hot property, and he was asked to participate in the arranger Gil Evans's second album as bandleader. Evans and Davis were already making plans to collaborate on Miles's next session, which would take place the following month.

Evans's idea was to dress up a handful of jazz standards with his own innovative and complex arrangements, which were recorded for Pacific Jazz, with the noted Columbia maven George Avakian producing. The effort, titled *New Bottle, Old Wine*, was cut in three sessions on April 9, May 2, and May 21. It featured a fourteen-piece orchestra, but Cannonball was clearly its star attraction. A year later Cannonball told *Melody Maker* magazine, "My big-band session with Gil Evans was indeed fulfilling. Gil has so much soul." In 1986 Evans told the historian Ben Sidran, "Cannonball played great on that album. Just the very opening he plays on 'St. Louis Blues,' it still gives me the chills."

Red Garland's abrupt exit from the *Milestones* sessions resulted in Davis's replacing him with pianist Bill Evans, who joined toward the beginning of May. The Sextet was currently ensconced at Café Bohemia while also making periodic appearances on the *Bandstand USA* radio program over WOR. Evans and Davis shared ideas about music often, with Evans introducing Miles to works by Maurice Ravel, Aram Khachaturian, and Sergei Rachmaninoff, among others. Drummer Philly Jo Jones was replaced by Cannonball's Florida friend Jimmy Cobb. Jones had struggled with a drug habit, and the constant problems it caused forced Davis to finally let him go the day before they were to record.

This version of the Sextet went into the studio on May 26 to record four songs, three of which would make up the B side of the album *Jazz Track*. ("Love for Sale" remained unissued until 1977.) Cannonball played on two of the three: "On Green Dolphin Street" (at his suggestion) and Miles's "Fran Dance" (listed on the original album jacket as "Put Your Little Foot Right Out"). The A side was reserved for Davis's atmospheric music for the film *Ascenseur pour l'échafaud*, recorded in Paris.

Several weeks later Cannonball recorded his first session for Riverside, a label for which he would record until the company's demise in 1964. Cannonball's relationship with Riverside would be the most successful, both musically and personally, in his career, thanks in great part to his respect for and his warm friendship with the producer Orrin Keepnews.

Keepnews and Riverside's co-founder Bill Grauer met while both were students at Columbia University. In December 1945 Grauer was hired to work as advertising manager for *The Record Changer*, an esoteric jazz collector's magazine that initially focused on traditional jazz. The dynamic, ambitious Grauer usually got what he wanted, and within two years he had purchased the magazine from its founder, Don Gullickson. Shortly after taking over, Grauer hired his friend Keepnews to contribute articles on contemporary jazz topics and named him managing editor.

With the advent of the long-playing record album, Grauer and Keepnews supported the efforts of independent record companies to reissue previously out-of-print historical jazz recordings from the 1920s on 78-rpm discs as well as the newer ten-inch LPs, despite the fact that the independent labels were pirating these recordings and issuing them without a proper license. A scandal resulted when Keepnews presented evidence, published in the November 1951 issue of *The Record Changer*, that RCA Victor, a vocal opponent of the pirate labels, was itself responsible for pressing bootlegs of its own product as well as that of Columbia on a pirate label brazenly called Jolly Roger Records. *The Record Changer* published reviews of these discs within its pages, many of them written by Keepnews. In an editorial in *Metronome* magazine titled "Rhythmic Thievery," George T. Simon accused Grauer and *The Record Changer* of encouraging and legitimizing bootleggers by giving them positive reviews in the magazine. Grauer responded by defending the bootleggers' practice and laying the blame squarely on RCA Victor and Columbia, who refused to reissue the material themselves in the first place.

A lawsuit waged by Louis Armstrong and Columbia Records resulted in the shutting down of Paradox Industries, the parent company of Jolly Roger; the pirating industry was silenced almost instantly. This did not, however, solve the problem of making the rare recordings available to the public. Grauer and Keepnews decided that if RCA Victor and Columbia would not reissue the historically valuable material from their own vaults, they would do so themselves. In the December 1952 issue of *The Record Changer*, Grauer announced the formation of Riverside Records (named for the company's New York telephone exchange) and his acquisition of the rights to the historically important Gennett, Champion, and

Supertone catalogs, which opened up the exciting anticipation of the first long-playing releases of vintage 78s by King Oliver's Creole Jazz Band, the State Street Ramblers, the Wolverines, and many more pioneering recordings from the 1920s.

In the same issue it was announced that RCA Victor had hired Grauer and Keepnews to produce a special series of reissues in their Vault Originals series on its newly formed X label. In 1955 Grauer sold *The Record Changer* in order to devote his full energies to Riverside. The label expanded from reissuing classic jazz 78s from the 1920s to exploring newer jazz forms such as bebop, signing forward-thinking artists such as Thelonious Monk, Randy Weston, and Mundell Lowe. Keepnews served as the label's producer, signing top artists from the burgeoning modern jazz scene.

Keepnews was introduced to Cannonball and Nat Adderley by a Riverside artist, trumpeter Clark Terry, on the street in front of Café Bohemia one evening in 1957. Cannonball was struggling with his Quintet at that time, but Keepnews liked the music the group was playing and tracked his activities for the next year. He was also impressed with the fact that Cannonball had his own personal manager, something that was not the norm in the jazz world in those days. Keepnews recognized immediately that EmArcy was doing Cannonball an injustice in having recorded his Quintet only once and then not even releasing those titles. In June 1958 Cannonball terminated his contract with Mercury and signed with Riverside. The signing marked a major turning point in his career. Up to that time, Cannonball's recordings were doing nothing for him, and the Quintet was losing money during engagements. Cannonball liked to joke that they were most successful when they weren't working because "at least we broke even."

Keepnews was delighted to sign Cannonball and his Quintet because he knew the saxophonist was a major creative talent as well as an outstanding individual. He later recalled:

Julian was one of the most completely alive human beings I had ever encountered. Seeing and hearing him on the bandstand, you realized the several things that went to make up that aliveness: he was figuratively and literally larger than life-sized; he was a multifaceted man and it seemed as if all those facts were constantly in evidence, churning away in front of you; and each aspect of him was consistent with every other part, so that you were automatically convinced that it was totally real and sincere, and you were instantly and permanently charmed.

He was a big man and a joyous man. He was a player and a composer and a leader, and when someone else was soloing, he was snapping his fingers and showing his enjoyment, and before and after the band's numbers, he talked to the audience (not talking at them or just making announcements), but really talking to them and saying things about the music, some serious, some very witty.

Cannonball's first Riverside session took place on July 1, 1958, at the Reeves Sound Studios in New York. Nat Adderley was still playing with J. J. Johnson, so Cannonball hired an old friend from Florida, Richard "Blue" Mitchell, to play trumpet. (At Cannonball's request, Keepnews flew to Miami to hear Mitchell play before hiring the band.) Mitchell had toured with Earl Bostic's band beginning in 1952; he'd then had a stint with Red Prysock before returning to Florida. To round out the Quintet, Cannonball used Bill Evans on piano, Sam Jones on bass, and Philly Joe Jones on drums. The album that ensued, titled *Portrait of Cannonball*, featured six songs, including one, "Nardis," that was written by Miles Davis especially for the group to record. Although Davis never recorded it himself, the song became associated with Bill Evans, who used it in his repertoire for the rest of his life. Davis's generosity in not only allowing Cannonball to sign a contract of his own while still playing with Miles's Sextet, but also presenting him with the gift of an original song to record, cannot be overstated.

Portrait of Cannonball is hard bop at its finest; in addition to "Nardis," the album also included Sam Jones's bass-driven "Blue Funk," saxophonist Gigi Gryce's "Minority," the (now obligatory) show tune "People Will Say We're in Love" from *Oklahoma!*, and two Cannonball originals: "Straight Life" (a new ballad featuring Mitchell playing lead and a particularly lush solo from Cannonball) and a remake of "A Little Taste" (first heard on Cannonball's debut effort for Savoy). The group was billed as the Julian Adderley Quintet, with a photograph of a coolly relaxed Cannonball, at ease and in charge, cigarette dangling from his lips, on the cover.

In his notes for the album, Keepnews addressed the fact that Cannonball had been bucking the "New Bird" appellation since his emergence on the scene in 1955, only to emerge as a confident leader with his own style. He also indicated that Cannonball was one of the few musicians who introduced his band and songs in lucid, audible English. Keepnews's noting of this aspect of Cannonball's personality would result in a bold experiment the following year that would cement Adderley's fame as a new kind of jazz musician, who didn't just play in front of an audience—he played *for* them.

Two days after his Riverside debut, Cannonball appeared with the Miles Davis Sextet at the Newport Jazz Festival. July 3 had been dubbed "Duke Ellington Night," but the Davis unit was the only band not to devote its set to Ellington works, choosing instead to present material it had been already performing. (Recordings of Davis's set were held back for release until 1964, when they were issued on the album *Miles and Monk at Newport* alongside a separate live appearance by Thelonious Monk.)

In its review of the concert, *Down Beat* noted, "Coltrane's playing has apparently influenced Adderley. The latter's playing indicated less concern for melodic structure than he has illustrated in the past." Upon release of the album six years later, a different perspective was presented by *Down Beat's* Pete Welding: "Adderley plays with assurance and bristling vigor, only occasionally reflecting Coltrane's turbulent manner." Turbulent was indeed the operative word for Charlie Parker's "Ah-leu-cha," on which Cannonball played a furious solo opposite the anarchic drumming of Jimmy Cobb. "Straight, No Chaser" had more of a propulsive groove than the slower version Cannonball had recorded for EmArcy earlier that year. Also included were versions of "Fran Dance" and "Two Bass Hit," both familiar numbers in Davis's set list.

Several weeks later Cannonball was back in the studio with Miles, but this time it was not with the Sextet; it was instead as an insignificant contributor to Davis and the arranger Gil Evans's concept album featuring big-band versions of songs from George and Ira Gershwin's opera *Porgy and Bess*. Davis initially decided not to use Coltrane and Cannonball on the album for fear that they would dominate Evans's saxophone section. Eventually the saxophones were eliminated altogether except for Cannonball's alto, with the other woodwind players playing clarinet, bass clarinet, flute, or alto flute. The rest of the players were studio musicians, except for Davis's regular bassist, Paul Chambers, and his former drummer, Philly Joe Jones.

While playing on the *Porgy and Bess* sessions, Cannonball participated in another ambitious project: John Benson Brooks's *Alabama Concerto*, a "bold fusing of jazz virtuosity, folk music themes, and what is usually called 'serious' composition." Brooks was a former big-band arranger who had toiled for Les Brown and Tommy Dorsey, among others, in the 1940s and had also written the hit song "You Came a Long Way from St. Louis." After the end of the big-band era, Brooks, who counted Evans among his close friends, embarked on more esoteric works, including *Folk Jazz, U.S.A.*, a 1956 album featuring saxophonists Zoot Sims and Al Cohn. The adventurous four-movement *Alabama Concerto*, Cannonball's second appearance on Riverside, was inspired by an anthropological field trip to Alabama conducted by the folklorist Harold Courlander. In the spirit of the Library of Congress's Alan Lomax, Courlander recorded contextual music in the African American community, including children's games, hollers, spirituals, work songs, lullabies, and blues. Brooks sought to correlate folk music with its influence on jazz, utilizing four musicians who could, as Keepnews stated in his album notes, "read like demons and blow like angels." The musicians he chose were Adderley, trumpeter Art Farmer, guitarist Barry Galbraith (who also played on *Folk Jazz, U.S.A.*), and bassist Milt Hinton, with Brooks himself playing piano in the third movement. Although the cover credits Adderley and Farmer as co-leaders, the album was marketed as Cannonball's.

One of the four movements focused on the legend of John Henry, a man-versus-machine story that was a popular topic in blues and folk repertoires. (Cannonball would tackle this subject on his own shortly before his death in 1975.) *Down Beat*'s Martin Williams praised Cannonball's performance on *Alabama Concerto*: "This, I believe, is Cannonball coming of age as an individual, purposeful, story-telling soloist."

On August 20 and 21 Cannonball recorded his last sessions for

EmArcy, an album in the spirit of the recently completed *Porgy and Bess* but devoted to Duke Ellington's 1941 musical *Jump for Joy*. Like *Porgy*, *Jump for Joy* decried the social plight of African Americans; but Ellington viewed *Porgy* as a production that emphasized stereotypes and caricatures and wanted to include more authentic language and costumes to go with the singing and dancing, without pandering to, as Barry Ulanov described it, the "white man's distorted idea" of what life was like for blacks in America.

Jump for Joy made its debut in Los Angeles. It featured a teenaged Dorothy Dandridge, blues singer Joe Turner, dancer and comedienne Marie Bryant, singer Ivie Anderson, and film star Herb Jeffries. The show was positively reviewed but ran for only three months and never made it to Broadway. Cannonball discussed the idea of recording songs from *Jump for Joy* with the Mercury producer Jack Tracy, who had the idea to create a concept album based on a common theme but at the same time wanted to avoid the usual tribute to show-tune writers such as Cole Porter or Rodgers and Hart. In the summer of 1958 *Jump for Joy* was dusted off and performed in a modernized version at Cops City in Miami, which was when it came to Cannonball's attention.

The album featured a jazz sextet—Cannonball on alto sax, Emmett Berry on trumpet, Bill Evans on piano, Barry Galbraith on guitar, Milt Hinton on bass, and Jimmy Cobb on drums—augmented by a classical string quartet. The arrangements were written by Bill Russo, who had created groundbreaking scores for the Stan Kenton orchestra in the 1950s. The idea to use strings was not another homage to the "Charlie Parker with Strings" concept that had been used so often in the 1950s (including Cannonball's own 1956 effort for EmArcy), but a way of recreating the emotional thrust of Ellington's original conception.

It had been a busy summer for Cannonball Adderley. In 1958 he had made great strides in his musical growth, thanks to the influences of Miles Davis and, especially, John Coltrane. He was looking forward to more creative work with his new label, Riverside, and was only too glad to put his disastrous contract with Mercury/EmArcy in his rear view mirror. Still, there were things gnawing at Cannonball that he would address in 1959, including his still burning desire to be a successful bandleader and team up again with his brother Nat. Before that could happen, however, one final album with Miles Davis would be recorded, an album that proved to be a touchstone in the history of jazz and one of the most famous albums of all time in any genre. In addition, Cannonball would suffer the first in a sequence of physical maladies that would prefigure his premature death less than two decades later.

6

KIND OF BLUE

The first evidence of Cannonball Adderley's chronic health problems came during a concert by the Miles Davis Sextet on September 9, 1958, that also served as a publicity event for Columbia Records. It was held in the Plaza Hotel's Parisian Room in New York and was recorded by Columbia. (The album was released as *Miles Davis: Jazz at the Plaza, Vol. 1* in 1973.) Reviewers noted that Cannonball's playing was not up to his usual level, but if Cannonball knew something was physically wrong with him, he didn't let on. The following week the Sextet played a weeklong engagement at Philadelphia's Showboat Jazz Theatre. Nat Adderley told Chris Sheridan, "His fingers stopped working for about twenty minutes while we were in the dressing room." By the time they returned to New York, Nat convinced his brother to check into a hospital for tests. Five weeks later a diagnosis of diabetes came in, but Cannonball told no one about it, not even Nat. (The examining physician was an old friend from Florida and kept Cannonball's secret.) Nat later found out that the doctors had given Cannonball three years to live if he did not change his diet and stop drinking. Cannonball was just about to turn thirty, but his body was already starting to break down. No one knows whether Cannonball would have lived longer had he acknowledged his condition, watched his weight and diet, and gotten plenty of rest. The fact that Cannonball was a trouper and thought first of everyone else but himself probably contributed to the worsening of his condition over the years.

On October 28 Orrin Keepnews set up a session for Cannonball to record an album for Riverside with vibraphonist Milt Jackson. The Quintet also included pianist Wynton Kelly (who would soon replace Bill Evans in the Miles Davis Sextet), bassist Percy Heath (who played with Jackson in the Modern Jazz Quartet), and Art Blakey. The album united Adderley and Jackson, both blues-minded players who weren't afraid to swing, and with Blakey providing the solid drumming, the group could have been called the MJQ Plus One.

One of Cannonball's gospel-inspired songs, the infectious "Things Are Getting Better," made its first appearance on an album. Jackson introduced the melody, which was derived from the jazz chestnut "Ja-Da." The soulfully upbeat mood of the song, and of the album in general, reflected the influence of the Adderleys' old FAMU bandmate Ray Robinson, now known as Ray Charles, the R&B star. Like Cannonball, he combined the feel of the church with a jazz sensibility on his albums for Atlantic Records. There is little doubt that Charles's records had as much of an influence on Cannonball as anything else he was listening to at the time and helped contribute to his future status as a jazz artist who could communicate with any audience, not just jazz aficionados.

As on many of his albums, the cover photo of Cannonball shows him in a joyful mood, hefting his King Super 20 Silversonic saxophone with one hand and beaming a smile a mile wide. The album title reflected the improvement of Cannonball's fortunes. He was now a star with Miles Davis and had a sympathetic producer at Riverside in Orrin Keepnews. Although his nascent health problems were worrisome, incidents were still few and far between and not serious enough to debilitate him.

As good as 1958 was for Adderley, 1959 would see him explode with a force that made his nickname that much more appropriate. It was in this year that he not only participated in the high-water mark of his stint with Miles Davis, but also solidified his style and finally broke through as a standout artist with potential crossover appeal.

The year 1959 started with Cannonball guesting on an album by trumpeter Kenny Dorham and a septet. Dorham had been a frontline partner with Charlie Parker, so the match was one that promised much bebop firepower. In keeping with his growing status, Cannonball's name was printed in the same font size as Dorham's on the cover of the Riverside album, titled *Blue Spring*. The novelty of the twelve-inch LP had worn off

By Kenny Dorham not Rodgers + Hart

by 1959, and producers were looking for other ways to entice buyers to sample their product. Unifying themes were often introduced, and with the album's release scheduled for the spring, Orrin Keepnews thought that "spring" would be the operative word for it. In keeping with this idea, five of the album's six songs had the word "spring" in their title, including show tunes by Rodgers and Hammerstein ("It Might as Well Be Spring") and Rodgers and Hart ("Spring Is Here" and "Passion Spring"). The remaining numbers were Dorham originals, including one play on words, "Spring Cannon," which featured you-know-who.

The septet configuration meant there was room for an extra horn, so baritone saxophonist Cecil Payne was added, a move that provided an additional punch to the proceedings. The first of two sessions took place on January 20, with Cedar Walton included on piano along with the stalwart Riverside rhythm section of Paul Chambers on bass and Philly Joe Jones on drums. (On February 18 Jimmy Cobb would replace Jones for the second day of the session.)

Meanwhile, the Miles Davis Sextet was displaying some fissures. Davis had no misconceptions about the longevity of this group, what with three potential bandleaders (Adderley, Coltrane, and Bill Evans) each maneuvering to go out on their own. Evans was tiring of the traveling and feeling uneasy about being the only white musician in the group (although Miles was color-blind in this regard). Evans also wanted to put some of his own ideas into practice. Before the end of the year, all three would leave Davis and start their own groups for different labels.

In addition to playing a subservient role to Davis, Cannonball had taken on the job of road manager, distributing payments to the musicians and keeping the books. Davis recognized that Cannonball had developed a good head for business since his EmArcy disaster and trusted him with the money the band was earning. For taking on this extra task Davis supplemented Cannonball's regular salary. But the agreement the two had come to was based on the assumption that Cannonball's position with Davis was only temporary. Initially it was supposed to have lasted a year, until Cannonball got back on his financial feet; but Davis convinced him to stay for a second hitch, and now that year was nearly half gone.

Evans was the first to leave, in November; Davis replaced him with Red Garland until he could find someone permanent. With Davis's help

Coltrane hired Harold Lovett to be his manager, who promptly got Trane a recording contract of his own with Atlantic. It was all Davis could do to keep Coltrane in his group to record one more album, which was scheduled to start recording in March.

On February 2, 1959, a group led by Paul Chambers held a recording session at the Vee-Jay studios in Chicago. The band was actually the Miles Davis Sextet, minus its leader. Davis had begun a two-week stint at the Sutherland Hotel and Lounge and had hired Wynton Kelly to be his new pianist, loaning out four of his band members (Chambers, Kelly, Cannonball, and Jimmy Cobb) to play the session. Replacing Miles on trumpet was the twenty-year-old prodigy Freddie Hubbard, who had been playing with the Montgomery brothers (Wes, Monk, and Buddy).

The band woke up the morning of the session to the news that three icons of rock and roll—Buddy Holly, Ritchie Valens, and the Big Bopper—had been killed when their small plane crashed a few minutes after takeoff while they were on their way from Clear Lake, Iowa, to their next gig in Moorhead, Minnesota—a result of poor weather conditions and the pilot's inexperience.

The Chambers album was completed that day. It was issued under the title *Go!*, and the album cover featured the image of a traffic signal with the green light illuminated. Later that day Cannonball, Kelly, Chambers, and Cobb walked down the hallway to record another session—Cannonball's last for Mercury—in an adjoining studio, with John Coltrane replacing Hubbard.

This album featured several blowing sessions that showcased Cannonball and Coltrane's "sheets of sound" approach, although it was by now easy to distinguish between the two, with Cannonball's solos the more melodic of the two and Coltrane's showing his signature technical bravado. Still, the chase choruses on such songs as "Limehouse Blues" and the Coltrane compositions "The Sleeper" and "Grand Central" resulted in some of the most exhilarating and thrilling moments on record.

The unique opportunity to land both Cannonball and Trane in one session was lost on Mercury and the producer Jack Tracy. Despite the presence of two of the most dynamic saxophonists on the jazz scene, this album, like all of the others featuring Cannonball, was placed on the shelf. It was released more than a year later as *Cannonball Adderley Quintet in*

Chicago to capitalize on Cannonball's own Quintet's overnight success with Riverside. Mercury's foresight proved to be myopic from the start to the finish of its ill-fated association with Cannonball Adderley.

On March 2, 1959, the Miles Davis Sextet went into Columbia's Thirtieth Street studios for the first of two days of recording that would result in what would become not only Miles's most celebrated album, but a watershed record in the history of jazz: *Kind of Blue.* Davis had been planning the album for some months and knew that he had better get into the studio and record while Cannonball Adderley and John Coltrane were still with the group. Bill Evans had already departed, but he had agreed ahead of time to do the album and participated in the session anyway, even though Wynton Kelly was now the band's permanent pianist. (Kelly would play on one of the tracks, "Freddie Freeloader.")

Davis's idea was to produce a new kind of jazz based on two specific elements. First, he would provide only musical sketches to his musicians, to encourage spontaneity. Second, he wanted to steer his music away from conventional Western harmonic structure and instead have his musicians improvise along modal lines rather than chord progressions. Only Davis and Evans were familiar with the written music; the other musicians not only had never seen the songs before, but were instructed to play them in an entirely new way. One song on the album *Milestones* ("Miles") had been approached in this fashion, but the songs Davis laid out for the Sextet to play on *Kind of Blue* were much more challenging. Davis wanted to achieve a sound geared more toward African and Eastern music, rather than Western. Davis and Evans had been listening intently to classical works, including Ravel's Concerto for the Left Hand and Orchestra and Rachmaninoff's Piano Concerto No. 4, both of which had an influence not only on their playing but even on their thinking.

In his autobiography Davis recalled that he was trying to recreate a memory from his childhood during a visit with relatives in Arkansas, when he would walk home from church with the sound of gospel music in his head. He was trying to achieve a sound that would replicate that of an African thumb piano, although in later years he expressed disappointment at not having been able to achieve the exact sound he wanted.

Three of the five songs that eventually made it to the *Kind of Blue* album were recorded that day: "Freddie Freeloader," "So What," and "Blue in

Green." "Freddie Freeloader" was named not for the hobo character created by television's Red Skelton, but for an anonymous acquaintance of Davis's who hung around the jazz scene, hoping for handouts. Davis wanted to record this song first so as not to upset Kelly, who was not pleased with Evans's presence on most of the album. Kelly's playing was perfectly suited for "Freddie Freeloader," as he was more accustomed to the cool twelve-bar blues form than Evans was. Miles's relaxed, open-horned solo was one of the finest of his career. Coltrane followed Miles with a fiery yet restrained solo of his own, and he in turn was followed by Cannonball, who was more comfortable with the blues idiom than any of the other musicians. A subdued musical conversation between Kelly and Chambers followed before the recapitulation of the theme completed the song. Five takes were recorded of "Freddie Freeloader," with the fourth take eventually making it to the final release (the others were false starts or incomplete performances). Miles Davis didn't like rehearsing or doing multiple takes, since they tended to spoil the spontaneity of a performance. During his two-year stint with Miles, Cannonball only recalled five instances where they actually prepared something—usually Coltrane demonstrating something to Cannonball.

"So What" got its title from an expression Miles Davis often used to dismiss pretentious criticism. With Evans now on piano, the piece began with an introduction provided by Gil Evans, an eerie, almost sinister duet between Evans and Chambers. The sequence was so quiet that the producer, Irving Townsend, complained that he could hear extraneous noises in the studio. Miles responded that the noises were part of a genuine jazz performance, but he allowed the musicians to start the song again. The melody was played by Chambers, with the horns answering with a two-note riff in classic call-and-response tradition. As on "Freddie Freeloader," Miles took the first solo, whose melancholy underpinning explains in part the album's title. What he was looking for was not necessarily a blues, but a "kind of blues," something that would evoke the same impressionistic response as the blues idiom did. In his understated fashion, Miles did not play flurries of notes; each was thought out and appropriately placed. In responding to Davis's solo, Coltrane followed with what was for him an equally taciturn sequence. Cannonball showed that he had adapted well to Miles's directions regarding modal harmonies but gave his solo definite blues inflections to go with his florid Coltrane-influenced runs. During Evans's solo, the horns played a shortened two-note riff on the upbeat rather than the downbeat, as in the initial sequence, before returning to the restatement of the original theme.

For the final song of the day, Evans's "Blue in Green," Davis had Cannonball lay out entirely. The song was designed as a subtle, delicate interlude between the funkier blues numbers on the album and was not particularly suited to Cannonball's style. Davis played it using his Harmon mute, with Evans's quiet piano behind him. Evans's solo is calming without being moody. Coltrane followed with an equally thoughtful break of his own. Miles's plan for this song was to play "sounds" instead of notes, and the lyrical beauty of "Blue in Green" fit perfectly in between the bold and playful "Freddie the Freeloader" and the moody but exotically flavored "Flamenco Sketches," which led off side 2 of the LP.

With that, the first day's recording came to an end. The group was supposed to reconvene on March 10, but the session was postponed for nearly a month to allow Cannonball's diabetes, which was flaring up again, to be treated. On April 6 they finally returned to the studio to complete the album. Scheduled were the two remaining songs, "Flamenco Sketches" and "All Blues." It's interesting that Davis would omit Cannonball from "Blue in Green" yet allow him to play on "Flamenco Sketches," even though it had a similarly melancholy, laid-back mood. Again, the opening was a call-and-response between Evans and Chambers before Davis, again using the Harmon mute, played the meandering, Spanish-flavored melody. The song foreshadowed the next project of Davis and Gil Evans, the monumental *Sketches of Spain* (by that time, however, both Coltrane and Cannonball had left the group). Coltrane's solo on "Flamenco Sketches" is lyrically beautiful, while Cannonball's somewhat brassier segment reflects the Spanish influence on the piece. Six takes of "Flamenco Sketches" were necessary, with the final one being accepted for release.

One number remained, "All Blues," which began with Chambers and Evans introducing the undulating 6/8 rhythm and the saxophonists playing the snakelike, gently swinging accompaniment. Davis introduced the melody, his trumpet again muted. When he came in for his typically economical solo, he discarded the mute, and the bluesy underpinning intensified, Cobb keeping time on his cymbal and providing offbeat accents on the snare. For the only time at the two sessions, Cannonball followed Davis with his solo, possibly because of his familiarity with the blues. Cobb kept his steady cymbal rhythm underneath Cannonball's solo, but his snare punctuations were less pronounced than on Miles's solo. After a preparatory drum roll by Cobb, Coltrane entered with a solo that showed signs of what was to come in the 1960s, when he all but abandoned rhythm and Western harmony for a totally free and new form of musical expression. Cobb followed along with pungent accents of each phrase until Evans came in to bring the song back down to earth. Three statements of the melody brought the song, and the album, to a satisfying finish, and Davis exhaled in ecstasy as the last note faded away.

When the session was over, Miles Davis was aware that his Sextet had produced a masterpiece. It was not necessary for years to pass before the importance of *Kind of Blue* would be realized not only by jazz critics but by the public as well. In the decades to come it surpassed even Davis's assessment. Today, it is the one jazz album that non-jazz fans have in their collections, and forty years after it was recorded it was still outselling all other jazz albums. It made people fall in love with jazz and, in turn, further explore the music played by its participants, especially John Coltrane and Cannonball Adderley, for whom *Kind of Blue* was their last musical association with Miles Davis. Miles had kept both of them around for this project knowing that it would have been impossible to execute it without them. *Kind of Blue* was a "perfect storm" jazz album: the perfect pieces in place at the right time in history. Although it was the creative peak of Miles Davis's career, Cannonball Adderley's star was still rising. Within the year, he would stage a comeback whose success would astound everyone in the jazz world except Cannonball himself.

7

CANNONBALL TAKES CHARGE

After the recording of *Kind of Blue*, Cannonball Adderley stayed on through the summer as a member of the Miles Davis Sextet, but the handwriting was on the wall. He was itching to resume his career as a bandleader, and Davis knew it. Still, there were gigs to play, and Cannonball had not yet decided in which direction he was going to go when he finally made the break. In the latter half of April 1959 the Sextet played a three-week gig at Birdland, during which time Cannonball participated in another Riverside album utilizing Davis's rhythm section of Wynton Kelly, Paul Chambers, and Jimmy Cobb. The session produced four of the seven songs that eventually would be issued as *Cannonball Takes Charge*. Cannonball was indeed taking charge of his future, and on the album he took advantage of his two musical strengths: the blues and his affinity for pop songs and show tunes.

The album led off with the exuberant "If This Isn't Love" from the Broadway musical *Finian's Rainbow*, Cannonball joyously and nimbly dancing through the number on his alto. A dreamy version of Jule Styne and Sammy Cahn's song "I Guess I'll Hang My Tears Out to Dry" followed, which showed off Cannonball's ability to play around the melody of a ballad without losing his audience. This kind of ability would help endear him to non-jazz audiences in the 1960s, and by this time Cannonball had that talent down pat.

"Serenata" was an unusual choice even for the hard-bop world of the late 1950s, in which astute musicians could cover anything from folk songs to children's nursery rhymes. "Serenata" was written by the highly esteemed composer and arranger Leroy Anderson, who wrote such instrumental classics of the 1950s as "Blue Tango" and "Sleigh Ride." "Serenata" was a Spanish-flavored romantic interlude, but Cannonball found its melody particularly conducive to jazz improvisation. (In 1960 Sarah Vaughan recorded a vocal version of the song that more closely approximated the feel of Anderson's original.) "I've Told Ev'ry Little Star" was a Jerome Kern–Oscar Hammerstein number published in 1932 and featured in the stage musical *Music in the Air*. With only a quartet, Cannonball had a rare opportunity to stretch out on an album that proved to be a showcase for his talents as a soloist.

Although he was feeling restless and chomping at the bit to return to his own band, Cannonball was happy that at last a record company was giving him room to do things on his own, instead of as a sideman or buried in a large orchestral setting, as EmArcy often did. These roles still fell to him on occasion—for instance, in a big-band session held in May led by Philly Joe Jones—but for the most part Riverside was keen on presenting Cannonball Adderley as a marketable star and kept him in the recording studio, sifting through personnel and looking for the right combination to support him. He knew that he wanted his brother Nat by his side again; the sax-and-cornet combination of the two Adderley brothers eventually defined his sound. But Nat was doing well on his own, playing lucrative gigs backing R&B artists.

The second session that comprised the *Cannonball Takes Charge* album took place on May 12, when Cannonball and Wynton Kelly used the brothers Percy (bass) and Albert (drums) Heath for their rhythm section. The three songs they recorded that day included the soulful "Barefoot Sunday Blues" (named by Keepnews) along with two standards that seemed unlikely for adaptation to jazz yet worked well when put in the hands of Cannonball Adderley: "Poor Butterfly," a 1916 chestnut that was inspired by Giacomo Puccini's opera *Madama Butterfly*, and the 1941 Johnny Mercer–Victor Schertzinger pop song "I Remember You."

By now, Cannonball was finally breaking free of the "New Bird" tag that he had been fighting since his appearance on the scene in 1955. The glowing reviews in *Down Beat* were now reflected by the magazine's readers. Upon the release of *Cannonball Takes Charge* that fall, an anonymous fan spoke for everyone when he gushed, "With this LP, Adderley firmly establishes his right to be called THE boss of the altos. [He] has gained an identity and individualism that none of the other neo-Parkerites has attained."

But despite the success of the album, Cannonball was still a sideman in the Miles Davis Sextet. His last gig with the group coincided with one of the most notorious incidents in Davis's career. It took place minutes after the band had completed a routine broadcast at Birdland for NBC's *Bands for Bonds* program. Birdland was the hot spot in New York to see jazz, with celebrities like Ava Gardner and Elizabeth Taylor coming out to see the show and greet the musicians afterward in their dressing room.

It was a hot, muggy, August night, and Davis was sweating after playing the broadcast. He had escorted a white girl to the curb outside the club, and they were waiting for a taxi when a policeman came along and told Davis to move on or he'd be arrested for loitering. Davis pointed to the Birdland marquee and told the cop who he was, but before he knew what was going on, he had been beaten and arrested for disorderly conduct and resisting arrest. Davis's cabaret card was revoked, and Nat Adderley had to be called in to replace him for the remainder of the gig.

After the engagement was over on September 2, Cannonball quit the band, and he and Nat went on tour with George Wein's Newport Jazz Festival Presents troupe using George Shearing's rhythm section. The tour began in Indianapolis and played subsequent concerts in Louisville, Chicago, Detroit, Boston, and Washington, D.C. before concluding in Philadelphia. While in Indianapolis, Cannonball went to the Missile Lounge to hear a young guitarist named Wes Montgomery. He was so impressed with Montgomery's performance that at intermission he called Orrin Keepnews and insisted that he arrange a recording session. Montgomery would become one of Riverside's star recording acts and a major force on the hard-bop scene of the 1960s. (Adderley would later record an album on Riverside with Montgomery.)

Davis made one last attempt to keep Cannonball in his Sextet, offering him a guaranteed annual salary of $20,000 to stay, but Cannonball knew the time was right for him to leave: while touring with Davis he noticed the response he was getting from audiences when his name was announced, and club owners had been asking him when he would be getting a band back together again. He began searching for a rhythm section that could support a front line consisting of himself on alto and Nat on cornet. Nat later told Chris Sheridan that his brother called his old Florida friend, bassist Sam Jones, who was then playing in Thelonious Monk's Quartet, and instructed him to get a rhythm section together because they were going to start playing right away in San Francisco. Jones called Louis Hayes, who was playing with Horace Silver, and got him to agree to play drums. Hayes was enthusiastic about joining the Adderleys but would not be available until early October. Now all they needed was a pianist. Junior Mance, who had played with the Adderleys in their first Quintet, was unavailable, having been hired to play with Dizzy Gillespie. But Jones knew that Cannonball wanted someone who could play soulful blues licks like Mance, so he called Bobby Timmons, who was currently playing with Art Blakey's Jazz Messengers.

The twenty-three-year-old Timmons joined Blakey in 1958 and was on hand when the Jazz Messengers recorded his composition "Moanin'" for Blue Note. Blakey had recorded for Blue Note before but had also made records for other labels. His return to Blue Note marked one of the earliest and most successful albums in the new genre known as hard bop, a combination of bebop infused with gospel and blues influences. The Blakey Quintet—which also included Lee Morgan on trumpet, Benny Golson on tenor sax, Jymie Merritt on bass, and the leader on drums—approximated what Cannonball Adderley had in mind for his group. Despite getting the musicians he wanted, Cannonball felt badly about taking Timmons and Hayes from bands led by Blakey and Silver, both of them friends of his.

The new Cannonball Adderley Quintet spent one day rehearsing before making its debut at Pep's Music Lounge in Philadelphia, where they played from September 22 to September 27. Because they had so little time to properly prepare, they played songs from the Quintet's first incarnation, including "Spontaneous Combustion," "Straight No Chaser" and adding Timmons's "Moanin'." After a few days off, they took off by automobile for San Francisco. It is possible that Cannonball made plans to open at San Francisco's Jazz Workshop with his new band as early as the summer, when the Davis Sextet was playing there. The club owner, Art Auerbach, had promised to book several weeks for him if he could have his own group ready by the fall.

On October 6, 1959, the new group made its debut at the Jazz Workshop, officially billed as Julian (Cannnonball) Adderley & the Quintet, featuring Nat Adderley. When a cannonball is shot from a cannon, the force behind it is such that nothing can stop it from reaching its target. Such was the musical force that was the Cannonball Adderley Quintet. Like a cannonball in flight, nothing could stop them now. The results were just as explosive.

8

SPONTANEOUS COMBUSTION

When the Cannonball Adderley Quintet arrived in San Francisco in the evening of October 4, 1959, Orrin Keepnews was there waiting for them. Keepnews knew the power Cannonball had over audiences. Cannonball had acted as the onstage spokesman for the Miles Davis Sextet, the withdrawn and taciturn Miles happy to remain in the background. Not only did Keepnews recognize Cannonball's gregarious, friendly way with his audiences; he also saw that the musician had intelligent things to say to listeners, cluing them on the background and makeup of the songs they were playing, introducing the band members, complimenting standout performances, cracking jokes, and speaking in a hip, casual manner that audiences could understand. The combination of the soulful musicianship and Cannonball's superlative onstage manner gave Keepnews the idea to record him in a live setting at the first opportunity. He told Cannonball that as soon as he felt ready to record, call him and he would be there, wherever it was. Keepnews thought that at the worst he'd have to go to Philadelphia to record, but when he finally got the call from Cannonball, it was to come to San Francisco, where the new Quintet was going to open at the Jazz Workshop on October 6. As there were no adequate recording facilities in the city, Keepnews decided to record a live concert at the club.

The Jazz Workshop was located at 473 Broadway in the North Beach district of San Francisco. North Beach was the equivalent of New York's Fifty-second Street, an area that was rife with nightclubs, strip joints, and late-night action. On any given night, one could go club hopping and hear the bawdy comedy of Lenny Bruce, folk revivalists the Kingston Trio, the blues of Lightnin' Hopkins, political raconteur Mort Sahl, the sibling comedy mayhem of the Smothers Brothers, and versatile jazz and blues singer Barbara Dane. In addition to the Jazz Workshop, jazz aficionados flocked to such clubs as El Matador, the Cellar, the Black Hawk, and Sugar Hill. To the eminent San Francisco jazz critic Ralph Gleason, the atmosphere at the Jazz Workshop during the Quintet's four-week gig was nothing short of magical.

By the time Keepnews arrived with his equipment, the Quintet was halfway through its four-week gig and had become the talk of the town. The Jazz Workshop had been doing capacity business, and on weekends it was next to impossible to get into the club. So many fans gathered on the street outside the club to hear the music wafting out onto the sidewalk that traffic was starting to be affected.

Inside, the atmosphere was electric. The irresistible rhythms and swinging solos, not to mention Cannonball's hip and witty introductions, connected with the audience in a way that was just extraordinary. No jazz musician had ever spoken to an audience the way Cannonball Adderley did. (Very few spoke at all.) At times a Cannonball Adderley show resembled a revival meeting rather than a jazz concert. The uninhibited reaction from the audiences was contagious, and the band fed off the enthusiasm to make their grooves even more captivating. Cannonball would later say, "I have never worked a job I enjoyed more."

One night the Russian composer Dmitri Shostakovich showed up to find out what the fuss was all about. It was his first American jazz concert. As Ralph Gleason related in his album notes, Shostakovich sat silently for an hour listening to the Quintet, smiled appreciatively several times, and even applauded vigorously on occasion, leaning forward to pay especially close attention to Louis Hayes's drum solos. Keepnews recognized the reaction the Quintet was getting from its audiences and wanted to capture that excitement live. The result was what he would later call "the birth of contemporary live recording."

The Adderley Quintet's album at the Jazz Workshop was far from the first successful attempt at capturing jazz live in concert. Primitive technology prevented many of the greats of early jazz from being recorded in concert settings, but with the advent of Benny Goodman's 1938 Carnegie Hall concert and Norman Granz's *Jazz at the Philharmonic* concerts, which began in 1944, jazz fans could experience the thrill and immediacy of a live jazz concert that had been captured on record. Many such efforts were committed to disc in the 1950s: Erroll Garner's *Concert by the Sea* (1955), the Dave Brubeck Quartet's *Live at Oberlin College* (1953), Sonny Rollins's *At the Village Vanguard* (1957), and, the most spectacular of all, *Duke Ellington at Newport* (1956), on which one can hear a galvanizing symbiosis of the performer-audience relationship, highlighted by Paul Gonsalves's epochal twenty-six-chorus saxophone solo on "Diminuendo and Crescendo in Blue."

But the era of live recording of jazz concerts would not start in earnest until after the success of *The Cannonball Adderley Quintet in San Francisco*, recorded on October 18 and 20, 1959. Keepnews, always thinking ahead, noticed that another Riverside artist, Thelonious Monk, was opening at the nearby Black Hawk, so after the second day of recording the Adderley Quintet he took his equipment to record Monk's group as well, just in case the Adderley gig didn't pan out.

The only part of the October 18 show that was included on the Adderley album was Cannonball's spoken introduction to the musical highlight of the record, Bobby Timmons's "Dis Here." In 1962 Cannonball recalled:

> Bobby Timmons wrote "Dis Here"—he used to say, "Dis here's my new tune"—in San Francisco, where we went after the first gig in Philadelphia. "Dis Here" fascinated me. I had never heard a tune like that before. It's a very difficult tune to play. Just playing the melody is tough. It was in 3/4 or 6/8, whichever way you want to look at it, and that made it challenging. It's got something in it to work on. At first, we had to force this tune on people, and they just wouldn't buy it. But the last week we were in San Francisco, it seemed as if almost magically some people started asking for it.

Keepnews insisted on starting the album with Cannonball's spoken introduction to "Dis Here," despite vehement objections by others at Riverside, including the label's owner, Bill Grauer. But Keepnews felt that Cannonball's personality was a big part of the Quintet's success and refused to cut any of Cannonball's asides and intros; later they would become one of the hallmarks of his success. His eighty-second intro to "Dis Here" was classic Cannonball:

> Thank you very much, ladies and gentlemen. Now it's time to carry on some. If we could have the lights out, please, for at . . . mos . . . phere . . . . Now, we're about to play a new composition by our pianist, Bobby Timmons. This one is a jazz waltz, however, it has all sorts of properties. It's simultaneously a shout and a chant, depending upon whether you know anything about the roots of church music and all that kind of stuff, meaning "soul" church music. I don't mean Bach chorales, that's different, you know what I mean? This is "soul," you know what I mean? All right. Now we're gonna play this by Bobby Timmons. It's really called "This Here," however, for reasons of soul and description, we have corrupted it to become "Dish, 'ere." So that's the name: "Dish, 'ere."

Timmons began the song with a piano riff, which was soon picked up by Hayes on the drums. Nat and Cannonball came in with the theme, which was played twice. Hayes's rhythm was quirky and off-kilter; it emphasized the second beat in each three-beat bar, giving the song an odd, lurching momentum. Cannonball's alto solo was swinging and funky, setting the pace for the other solos to follow—first Nat on cornet, then Timmons on piano, with Cannonball and Nat picking up on the piano riff and playing behind him. The intensity heightened, and Cannonball urged Timmons on by clapping along on Hayes's second beat. The Adderleys finished the song by restating the melody, and after eleven minutes the tune finally ended, whereupon the crowd erupted in wild cheers. "Dis Here" became so popular that Riverside issued a truncated version of it on two sides of a 45-rpm single. It was soon selling as many copies as the entire album, proving that there was crossover appeal for the new Quintet.

It was probably Grauer who came up with the term, "soul jazz," with which he marketed the music of the Cannonball Adderley Quintet. Nat Adderley believed that it was around this time that the word "soul" first became connected with black musicians. He explained that the definition of soul did not always refer only to blacks; the way he saw it, a musician played with soul if he could swing without a rhythm section's support. He said musicians should be able to feel each beat of a musical bar just by the way pulses are played and felt.

In the 1950s black jazz musicians found themselves being displaced in favor of whites from the West Coast. People such as Chet Baker, Stan Getz, and Gerry Mulligan were getting all the jobs, while black musicians like Blakey, Horace Silver, and even Miles Davis were not. About this time the word "soul" became associated solely with the gospel church, attended primarily by blacks. The label "soul" or "soul jazz" implied that these musicians possessed something the white musicians could not. In explaining this theory, Nat emphasized that he did not agree with this new meaning of "soul" but observed that the public was being fed this label as being equated with black musicians.

Cannonball had not recorded "Spontaneous Combustion" since his first solo effort for Savoy in 1955. The Riverside version, led off by Sam Jones's bass, was taken at a faster tempo and swung just as hard as "Dis Here." On the recording, one can hear Cannonball urging Nat on during his solo with shouts of "Yeah, yeah, yeah!" and "All right!" Then Timmons kicked things into high gear with his solo, which really got the club rocking. The song concluded with a rousing chase chorus by the Adderley brothers, which brought an ovation from the crowd. If ever there was a perfect name for the effect the Cannonball Adderley Quintet had on the Jazz Workshop audience that night, it was "Spontaneous Combustion."

The album cover featured a photograph of Cannonball and Nat in front of a wall that had been covered with a red wallpaper design; Keepnews thought it looked like it belonged in San Francisco. Cannonball is standing over Nat, with his hand affectionately placed on his brother's shoulder. Nat, who is seated on a chair, is looking up at him. Cannonball appears to be explaining something to Nat, who looks amused, his cornet resting on his right knee. It was an informal shot that beautifully summed up the Adderleys' close relationship. Despite being the leader of the band, Cannonball gave his brother the credit "featuring Nat Adderley" whenever he could, and the cover of the album included this phrase.

In those days jazz musicians carried a stigma of which Cannonball Adderley was keenly aware. The public had been made to view the stereotypical jazz musician as being either a goateed bopster (like Dizzy Gillespie), a junkie (like Charlie Parker), or a professorial type with horn-rimmed glasses (like Dave Brubeck). In any case, jazz musicians of the 1950s were viewed as self-involved and unapproachable. They spoke their own hipster language and played complex music that few listeners could relate to. Cannonball Adderley changed all this by letting the audience in. He addressed them directly with respect and treated them as if they were his friends. He didn't preach to them, but he did explain in often humorous ways what they were going to be listening to, who wrote the song, who was playing in the band, and even how the songs got their titles. Ralph Gleason wrote in the liner notes that he had never seen anything like the response the Quintet got from the San Francisco crowd, a response born of the warmth and affection that developed between Adderley and his audience.

In addition, Cannonball and his bandmates were clearly having fun—cheering each other on, making comments of affirmation during solos, and "digging the grooves." Cannonball would snap his fingers while Nat or Timmons was playing a solo, or rotate his right arm. The latter gesture became something of a signature move that would turn audiences on and have them cheering. The whole experience was something that had been more or less absent from live jazz performance during the bebop era. The Cannonball Adderley Quintet had made jazz accessible.

A good portion of the *Jazz Workshop* album's success can probably be credited to the New York disc jockey "Symphony Sid" Torin, who hosted an all-night jazz program on WEVD. Torin was known for his championing of Afro-Cuban jazz and hard bop, and he was a faithful promoter of New York jazz artists. Lester Young wrote the song "Jumpin' with Symphony Sid" in honor of Torin's efforts, and "vocalese" singer King Pleasure later added lyrics to Young's improvised solo. After the *Jazz Workshop* album was released, Torin played it constantly on his program, and by the time Adderley's Quintet returned to New York in late November, after having played gigs in Denver and Chicago, it was a runaway hit.

On December 3, after a week at Birdland, the band began a two-week engagement at the Village Gate. Huge crowds awaited the group there, with everyone screaming for "Dis Here" and the other songs from the *Jazz Workshop* LP. *Down Beat* reported that the group "caused a near riot"—the club was packed with "jazz fans and assorted beatniks, all of whom were reacting with enthusiasm to Cannonball's alto and Nat's mellow horn."

Although Monday was normally the band's night off during their weeklong gigs, the Village Gate engagement was so popular that Cannonball was called upon to play at Pete Long's weekly Monday night jazz concerts at the club.

Within a year, *Cannonball Adderley at the Jazz Workshop* sold eighty thousand copies, a phenomenal number for a jazz album and one that earned the group a gold record. In addition, Cannonball received his first award as best altoist in both the *Down Beat* Critics Poll and its Readers Poll. Writing in the *New York Times*, the jazz critic John S. Wilson was impressed with the progress Cannonball had made as a musician: "In the past, Mr. Adderley has been noted for his ability to weave endless beautifully executed lines at torrential tempos that signified practically nothing. During the past year or two, particularly while he was a member of Miles Davis' group, he appears to have been going through a period of self-appraisal." Wilson went on to praise the revived Adderley Quintet's "down home" sound, which came as a result of stylings adopted from the Horace Silver Quintet, augmented by "conditioning elements" from Miles Davis: "In these surroundings the playing of both Adderley brothers has taken on a firmness and shape that it has lacked in the past and, in the process, has acquired much more meaning. The entire group expresses itself with great warmth and with an intensity that suggests that every man is really involved in his playing."

The overwhelming success of the *Jazz Workshop* album gave the Adderleys encouragement to craft new compositions to suit their equally new unit. They began 1960 with successful engagements in Chicago and Washington, D.C., then returned to New York to play for three weeks at the Half Note. Anxious to record again, Keepnews set up a studio session for the Quintet. Art Blakey had been pressuring Bobby Timmons to return to the Jazz Messengers, and Keepnews wanted to take advantage of the success of "Dis Here" by recording a follow-up song by Timmons titled "Dat Dere."

The Quintet entered the Reeves Sound Studios on February 1, 1960, to record half of what would be called *Them Dirty Blues*. In addition to "Dat Dere," the session introduced a new composition by Nat Adderley that would become an even bigger hit than either of the Timmons tunes and one of the anthems of the soul-jazz movement. The number, titled "Work

Song," did not reach its final form until the group's next session, which wouldn't take place for nearly two months.

By this time the band had gotten so hot that Keepnews had to chase them halfway across the country to get them to hold another session to complete the album. The Adderley Quintet was the hottest jazz combo in the nation, with gigs beginning to be lined up for the rest of the year.

Cannonball used his newfound fame to become a stockholder in the Communicating Arts Corporation, a group formed by three junior executives with United Artists Records whose goal was to create a solid block of jazz radio programming for New York City. The station they selected, WNCN-FM, would devote five hours of jazz programming daily, from 10 P.M. to 3 A.M. The on-air hosts included the journalists Ira Gitler, Nat Hentoff, and Martin Williams, with Adderley spinning discs and conducting interviews on Friday nights from eleven until midnight.

With Adderley leading the way, the hard-bop movement had gathered up a full head of steam and was now a roaring juggernaut. Artists such as Horace Silver, Jimmy Smith, Lou Donaldson, and Ramsey Lewis were among those who started enjoying increased attention in the wake of the *Jazz Workshop* album. A new era had been launched. Jazz, America's most resilient form of music, had mutated again, absorbing the soulful sounds espoused by such acts as Ray Charles, the Staple Singers, and Charles Brown, mixing musical styles in the same manner that produced rock and roll a few years earlier. Whereas bebop never gained more than a finite, esoteric audience, Cannonball Adderley had moved beyond it and was now rising above the waves into the mainstream of popular music. Like jazz itself, the 1960s would prove exciting for the country, but also tumultuous.

9

WORK SONG

Despite the success of *The Cannonball Adderley Quintet in San Francisco*, it was a song on the group's follow-up album that had a more lasting effect on their growing popularity. "Dis Here" had become the band's most popular song and was requested wherever they went, but their crossover appeal really didn't become cemented until they released their next album, *Them Dirty Blues*. This record featured not only Timmons's sequel "Dat Dere," but also a song that changed the way jazz was perceived by the general public in the 1960s: Nat Adderley's "Work Song."

Before "Work Song," the instrumentals of bebop bands featured melodies that were either ridiculously brief or complex and obtuse and hard to follow. Many songs in the early years of bebop were based on chord changes to older popular songs such as "I Got Rhythm" or "Whispering," and the melodies were often viewed as an afterthought by the musicians, who just wanted to take off and improvise on the chord changes. As time went on, jazz musicians wrote songs, like Charlie Parker's "Ornithology" or "Au Privave," that had complicated melodies and that the average listener found anything but singable. With "Work Song," the Cannonball Adderley Quintet reintroduced to jazz the concept of an easily remembered melody, something that Duke Ellington had pioneered in the 1920s and 1930s and that made the song more accessible to the mainstream popular-music market.

The sixteen-bar melody of "Work Song" is memorable, catchy, and easily sung, with a beginning, a middle, and a satisfying end. Like "Dis

Here," "Work Song" was issued as a 45-rpm single and became a popular jukebox hit. The 1960s would become the high-water mark for jazz instrumentals played on mainstream radio stations, with artists such as the Ramsey Lewis Trio ("The In Crowd"), Chris Barber ("Petite Fleur"), and Herbie Mann ("Memphis Underground") all enjoying crossover hit status with popular singles.

In an interview, Nat Adderley recalled that his inspiration for "Work Song" came from a childhood experience. One day he saw a group convict laborers paving the street in front of the Adderley home in Florida. While they worked, their leader sang a melody, and the other inmates would respond. As a young boy, Nat had no clue that these men were prisoners being punished for doing something that was against the law; he just enjoyed their music. Unlike other songs written about chain or work gangs, "Work Song" did not replicate the rhythm of the workers' toil, such as the songs by blues singer Huddie "Lead Belly" Ledbetter. Its melody simply reminded Nat of the one this particular group sang while working in front of his parents' house.

"Work Song" was so singable that a young songwriter from Chicago named Oscar Brown Jr. decided it would be appropriate to add lyrics to it. This wasn't the first time words had been put to a jazz instrumental, but it happened at a particular point in jazz history when the pop world was ready to accept a jazz composition as a piece of popular music, especially when it was conveyed by an affable, friendly, and congenial bandleader who enjoyed his audiences as much as they enjoyed him.

Oscar Brown Jr. started writing lyrics as a hobby when he was growing up in Chicago in the 1930 and '40s. In an interview, he explained how he created lyrics to jazz compositions. One of his first was Duke Ellington's "What Am I Here For?" Later on, after he entered the army, he heard Thelonious Monk's "'Round Midnight" and started experimenting with lyrics for other songs in the new bebop genre. He became more and more comfortable with the process and asked jazz musicians whether they had any instrumentals that might work with a set of lyrics. When Cannonball Adderley's recording of "Work Song" became popular, Brown had just signed a contract to record for Columbia Records as a solo artist. He asked Cannonball and Nat for permission to write a set of lyrics for it. After discussing the matter, Cannonball and Nat agreed to let Brown give it a try. Nat told Brown the story about the Florida chain gang, which was all Brown needed to write the lyrics:

> *Breakin' up big rocks on uh chain gang*
> *Breakin' rocks an' servin' my time.*
> *Breakin' rocks ou' chere on the chain gang*
> *'Cause I been convicted of crime.*

> *Chorus:*
> *Hol' it steady right there while I hit it.*
> *There! I reckon that oughta git it*
> *Been workin' an' workin'*
> *But I still got so terrible long to go!*

Brown's version of "Work Song" was included on his first Columbia LP, *Sin and Soul . . . and Then Some*, released in 1960. The album was a smash hit, bringing the music of the Adderleys to a completely different audience.

Brown would find other jazz instrumentals that were suited for lyrics. The most famous of these was Miles Davis' "All Blues," whose lyrics Brown penned while he was on an airplane looking out the window at an endless blue sky. The songs on *Them Dirty Blues* included "Work Song" as well as two other songs for which Brown supplied lyrics. To Brown, Bobby Timmons's "Dat Dere" suggested the kind of endless questioning Brown was getting from his four-year-old son. The hipster words "Dat Dere" had now become the endearing nonstop language of an inquisitive little boy just learning to talk:

> *Hey, daddy, what dat dere*
> *'N' why dat under dere*
> *'N' oh, daddy, oh, hey, daddy hey look it ober dere.*
> *Hey, where dey goin' dere?*
> *'N' what dey do in dere?*
> *'N' daddy, can I ha' dat big elephunt ober dere?*

Timmons, who also had a boy the age of Brown's son, loved the song. Duke Pearson's reaction to Brown's lyrics for his composition "Jeannine" was another matter entirely. Like Brown's "Dat Dere," "Jeannine" was a playful song that Pearson had written about his own six-year-old niece, but after Brown got through with it, Jeannine had become a sophisticated, swinging gold digger.

> *Last time, last time I saw Jeannine*
> *She looked just like a royal queen*
> *As she cruised by with some wealthy guy*
> *In some Cadillac limousine,*
> *Last time I saw Jeannine.*

When Pearson learned that Brown had changed his tribute to his little niece to something entirely different, he was annoyed and refused to acknowledge the new lyrics. After Pearson's death in 1980, his parents gave their blessing to Brown's publisher, Upam Music Co. But Brown himself recorded the song on his 1963 Columbia album, *Tells It Like It Is*.

On January 27, 1960, five days before Cannonball Adderley began recording *Them Dirty Blues*, Nat Adderley assembled his own group to record an album for Riverside. The band included Bobby Timmons on piano, Wes Montgomery on guitar, Percy Heath on bass, and Louis Hayes on drums. Sam Jones alternated with Heath on bass but also played cello on several sides, including the first recording of "Work Song." On February 1 Timmons, Jones, and Hayes joined the Adderley brothers in the studio for another version of "Work Song," along with "Dat Dere," the Gershwin number "Soon" (which Cannonball had recorded with Sarah Vaughan in 1955), and Sam Jones's "Del Sasser."

After a performance at the Half Note in New York on February 21, Bobby Timmons gave his notice, telling Cannonball that he was returning to Art Blakey's Jazz Messengers. Timmons had been unhappy about his earnings from "Dis Here" and decided to leave when Blakey offered him more money to return to his group. Undeterred, Cannonball (who may have anticipated this move) brought in Detroit-based Barry Harris to replace Timmons on piano. The band took four weeks off while Harris learned their repertoire, and the group made their debut with their new pianist at Curro's in Milwaukee, Wisconsin, on March 21. On March 29 the Quintet completed the songs designated for *Them Dirty Blues*, which included the title track, "Jeannine," another version of "Work Song," and

"Easy Living" (a pop song from the 1937 film of the same name, written by Ralph Rainger and Leo Robin). It was this version of "Work Song," featuring Barry Harris, that was eventually released on the album. (The earlier recording with Timmons was eventually issued on a Landmark LP in 1985.)

In May the Quintet made a triumphant return to the Jazz Workshop in San Francisco, where they played to turn-away crowds. Meanwhile Orrin Keepnews discovered that two other major bands were playing gigs at the same time in the Bay Area—at the Black Hawk the other major San Francisco jazz venue, the Ray Brown Trio; and across the bay in Oakland, guitarist Wes Montgomery, who had been discovered by Cannonball and was starting a new group with his brothers Buddy and Monk.

Adderley, Montgomery, and Brown were all recent winners of the major jazz magazines' annual readers' and critics' polls, so Keepnews formed a unique quintet centering on Cannonball, Brown, and Wes Montgomery. Completing the group were Cannonball's regular drummer, Louis Hayes, and the twenty-six-year-old British vibraphonist Victor Feldman, who had been playing in Los Angeles when Cannonball called him. Cannonball's idea was to feature Montgomery and Brown on the album, and he thought the vibraphone would make an ideal balance for the sound.

Feldman fit perfectly into Cannonball's soulful vibe. Of the three songs recorded on May 21, two were penned by Feldman, "The Chant" and "Azul Serape." The other was a Barry Harris tune called "Lolita." The recordings were cut at a side-street theater in North Beach called Fugazi Hall that was locally known for its series of poetry readings for the beat generation. Keepnews dubbed the group and the album *Cannonball Adderley and the Poll-Winners.*

Two weeks later they reassembled at United Studios in Los Angeles to record the three last songs for the album. Keepnews had returned to New York to attend to Riverside's other activities and left Cannonball in charge of producing the session. Despite the stellar accomplishments of the individual poll winners, *Down Beat*'s Don DeMichael was not impressed, reporting that the group sounded "like a gathering of strangers."

With summer came the annual festival season, and the Adderley Quintet returned to the Newport Jazz Festival, where Cannonball also played with the Newport Youth Orchestra. The concert was filmed for the U.S. Information Service and released under the title *Jazz USA*. The Quintet's performance later that day (June 30) was warmly reviewed by John S. Wilson in *Down Beat*, who called it "a roaring session of crisply urgent, vigorous blowing."

On July 26 Cannonball participated in what may have been the strangest recording session of his career: a cameo appearance with the Nutty Squirrels. In 1958 the inventive composer Ross Bagdasarian recorded a runaway hit called "Witch Doctor," whose gimmick was a speeded-up voice singing a nonsense refrain that anyone growing up in that year can probably still sing without effort a half century later ("Oo, ee, oo ah ah, ting, tang, walla walla bing bang").

A sequel of sorts to "Witch Doctor" was "The Chipmunk Song," issued in time for the holiday season, which featured three of these electronically manipulated, harmonizing voices representing a trio of chipmunk siblings named Alvin, Simon, and Theodore. Bagdasarian gave himself a pseudonym, "David Seville," and the resulting song took its place alongside hula hoops, poodle skirts, and the Edsel as iconic elements of 1950s America. (The record inspired several albums of similar material, an animated cartoon series, and a veritable industry that has lasted to this day, with Bagdasarian's son carrying on the tradition.)

To capitalize on the Chipmunk phenomenon, the jazz musician Don Elliott and the TV composer Alexander "Sascha" Burland decided to combine the Chipmunk vocal effect with the sound of the reigning jazz vocalese trio, Lambert, Hendricks & Ross. Bagdasarian was struggling to bring his Chipmunks to the television screen, but Elliott and Burland beat them to it, creating a hipper, jazzier group called the Nutty Squirrels and mounting an animated television program of their own. The Nutty Squirrels came out with their own catchy single, the two-part "Uh-Oh," which crashed *Billboard* magazine's pop singles chart in the fall of 1959. (The B side actually made it to no. 14.) An accompanying LP was issued on the tiny Hanover label.

The Nutty Squirrels became so popular that the "group" was signed to record a sequel LP for Columbia Records, for which Lambert, Hendricks & Ross recorded. The album, titled *The Nutty Squirrels Go Bird Watching*, included jazz songs with an avian theme, such as "Flamingo," "Skylark," and "When the Red, Red Robin Comes Bob, Bob, Bobbin' Along."

Cannonball Adderley appeared on one track on the album, Charlie Parker's "Yardbird Suite."

The success of the Cannonball Adderley Quintet's Riverside albums resulted in an increase in bookings as well as requests for Cannonball to appear at a variety of other musical events. He supervised the Riverside album featuring the Mangione Brothers, Chuck and Gap, who would become major influences in the 1970s jazz scene. It was at that session that Cannonball became acquainted with Roy McCurdy, who would later become his regular drummer.

By the summer of 1960 it was becoming apparent that jazz was changing. Bebop was now considered passé, and hard bop and soul jazz were beginning to be recognized as the new direction the genre was taking with the approach of the new decade. Inevitably, the keepers of the old guard began to resent the popularity of Cannonball Adderley and those who did not adhere strictly to the old bebop formulas. One of these was the jazz critic Ira Gitler, who sneered that Adderley's music was "overfunk."

The respected jazz bassist Charles Mingus was also no fan of Adderley's music. In the July 21 issue of *Down Beat*, he called Adderley "Rock-n-roll musician No. 1" and claimed that the Adderley Quintet's recording of "Dis Here" plagiarized his own "Better Git It in Your Soul," which had been featured on Mingus's Columbia album *Mingus Ah Um*. (Other than both being in triple meter, there is little resemblance between the two numbers. The Mingus track is actually closer to Elmer Bernstein's theme song for the film *Walk on the Wild Side* than to Bobby Timmons's work.)

Nat Adderley took Gitler, Mingus, and other critics to task in the August 4 issue of *Down Beat*, wondering why people had started resenting his brother now that he was becoming successful. "We're not making that much money," he explained. "Cannon is the only leader I ever knew who told a club owner he was offering us too much money because he didn't want to see the club go out of business through overpaying." Nat went on to describe how he and his brother grew up listening to the music in the Tabernacle Baptist Church across the street from their home. "People get the idea that this kind of feeling can be contrived. It can't. Hell, I lived with it all my life. I happen to be a part of the social scene of the south. Cannonball and I play the way we feel it."

After analyzing the styles of various jazz trumpeters and Mingus's own style, Nat went after those he called "hypocritical critics," the ones who started putting Cannonball down as soon as he started attracting larger audiences. He accurately projected that in the decades to come, musicians such as Dave Brubeck, another trailblazer who had drawn the ire of critics after becoming popular, would be viewed as jazz giants.

Nat Adderley, who had earned a degree in sociology at Florida A & M, pointed out that because of jazz's curious in-group appeal, certain insiders "will reject an artist when he gains widespread appeal because he can no longer serve as a symbol of their exclusiveness." As for Mingus, Nat postulated that no jazz musician could claim exclusivity for tunes written in 3/4 time, just as no one could appropriate the blues or gospel as his own. "J. J. Johnson has been doing 3/4 things for a long time," he wrote. Then he challenged Mingus to sue them if he thought Timmons and Cannonball had conspired to plagiarize his song.

Criticisms from Gitler, Mingus, and others only persisted as Cannonball Adderley continued his crossover success in the 1960s. Although Cannonball shrugged off these accusations, he was conscious of the criticism. A former teacher, he used his knowledge of jazz history to engage some of his adversaries in conversation about his music, even participating in a "debate" between musicians and critics that took place at the New York apartment of Miles Davis. The panel, moderated by the press agent Peter Long, was made up of Cannonball Adderley, J. J. Johnson, Horace Silver, Miles Davis, and Gerry Mulligan.

In the summer of 1960 Cannonball was commissioned to organize and lead a seventeen-piece big band to play at the fifth annual Randall's Island Jazz Festival, held at an East River playground that was used mostly for track meets and soccer matches. At the previous festival, held in 1959, some sixty thousand fans had packed the stadium, making it an even larger event than the Newport Jazz Festival.

The 1960 edition promised a dizzying array of all-stars, including Miles Davis, Herbie Mann, Count Basie, Dizzy Gillespie, Duke Ellington, John Coltrane, and dozens more. Cannonball's orchestra, which performed on August 20, was anchored by his own Quintet, augmented by musicians that included Clifford Jordan and Clark Terry. Jimmy Heath was hired to pen new arrangements of Adderley standards, including "Bohemia after Dark" and "Dis Here."

After a weeklong engagement at New York's Basin Street East nightclub, pianist Barry Harris decided to resign from the Quintet. Harris never felt that his style suited the group; he was interested in forming a trio and playing New York clubs rather than touring the country with Cannonball. Adderley remembered the Englishman Victor Feldman, who had meshed so well with the group on the *Poll-Winners* LP, and cabled him in Los Angeles with an offer to join the Quintet. Feldman joined the group in September at the Monterey Jazz Festival and was also on hand when the Quintet was a guest on *The Debbie Reynolds Show* a few days later—the first modern jazz group to play on a coast-to-coast television program. (They played, unsurprisingly, "Dis Here.") The telecast increased demands for appearances by the Quintet, and Riverside was almost overwhelmed by a surge in sales for its 45-rpm single version of "Dis Here," which had now sold some 75,000 copies.

On October 16, 1960, the Quintet was recorded in concert at a legendary Los Angeles nightclub, Howard Rumsey's Lighthouse in the suburb of Hermosa Beach, fifteen miles south of downtown Los Angeles— the cradle of West Coast jazz. The resulting album represented the crest of Cannonball Adderley's career. He was never more popular than he was at the beginning of 1961, and his musical accomplishments began to be augmented by other activities that reflected some of the goals Cannonball had been striving toward since his earliest days in music: spreading the popularity of jazz and participating in concerts benefiting the civil rights movement.

10

A VERY IMPORTANT CAT

B y the fall of 1960 the Cannonball Adderley Quintet had become so popular that rival labels were searching their archives for Adderley material so that they could capitalize on his success. World Pacific's Dick Bock packaged a 1958 session by Gil Evans as an Adderley album (*New Bottle, Old Wine*), with Cannonball's name printed in larger type than Evans's on the cover even though Cannonball was only a featured soloist. Upon complaints from Bill Grauer, owner of Riverside Records, Bock pulled the album from the market until the cover could be more accurately designed.

Mercury Records, whose recalcitrance had led Cannonball to leave the label, now decided that he was marketable and took a 1958 session by the Miles Davis Sextet (sans Miles) and titled it *The Cannonball Adderley Quintet in Chicago*. (Unlike World Pacific, Mercury did not pull this album; they used it in a variety of reissues over the ensuing years.)

Anticipation over the Cannonball Adderley Quintet's forthcoming encore live album at the Lighthouse was so great that Riverside Records received advance orders in excess of 50,000 units. Although the in-studio *Them Dirty Blues* album was successful, it didn't stir the public's excitement as much as the live *In San Francisco* album did, so for Orrin Keepnews the message was clear: live albums were what fans wanted from Cannonball Adderley. The audience's reaction had become an integral factor in Cannonball's albums, reflecting the magical relationship Cannonball had with them, a relationship that channeled their enthusiasm directly into the records' grooves. Keepnews also had come to the conclusion that

Cannonball's spoken introductions had become his trademark, and he made it a point to include them in any future live albums.

The concert was a one-day engagement at Howard Rumsey's Lighthouse. Since the date fell on a Sunday, Keepnews would be able to take advantage of five full sets, including a matinee, from which he would draw the takes needed for the album. This would also be the first album featuring Feldman, the group's new pianist, who contributed two songs (the Latin-flavored "Azul Serape" and "Exodus") to the session. The hit of the album, however, was another "funky finger-snapper," Cannonball's "Sack o' Woe," which Cannonball introduced on the album as having a rhythm that was conducive for dancing. (A truncated version of the ten-minute-long track was extracted for a two-part 45-rpm release on Riverside.)

In November the producer and founder of Verve Records, Norman Granz, invited the Quintet to join one of his *Jazz at the Philharmonic* package tours of Europe. Concerts were held in Holland and Sweden before they moved on to Germany, France, and, finally, the United Kingdom. Granz issued some of the material on his Pablo label many years later—in 1984, tracks from the Swedish dates, and in 1997, those from a Paris performance. At the latter, Granz introduced the band in French, but when Cannonball came on, he was noticeably embarrassed at not being able to communicate with the audience. When he cracked a joke about the origins of the song "Jeannine" ("It was done for a friend of mine who was very talented, and her name was Jeannine, so that always helps") and got no response, he got flustered and said, "I wish I could speak French, so you could . . . you know what I mean, so there it is," and immediately cued Victor Feldman to launch into the introductory riff for "Dis Here." Still, the recordings captured the enthusiasm of the European audiences to the Quintet's music, even without Cannonball's hip and lucid introductions.

As 1961 dawned, Orrin Keepnews decided to take advantage of Cannonball Adderley's conversational skills by having him narrate *A Child's Introduction to Jazz*, an album issued on Riverside's subsidiary children's label Wonderland. With a script written by Keepnews, the record proposed to demonstrate not where jazz came from but how it sounded, starting with Riverside's massive vault of vintage 78s dating back to the 1920s and progressing to include portions of Cannonball's own recordings for the label. The album was supposed to be expanded into a television program paralleling Leonard Bernstein's classical music series, the *Young People's Concerts*, but it apparently never got off the ground. Nevertheless, Cannonball used the album as a focus for a series of concerts the Quintet staged in high schools and community centers, something he enjoyed doing for the rest of his life.

Cannonball expanded into other activities as well, beginning with his lifelong promotion of civil rights for African Americans. In September 1960 Cannonball and the actor Brock Peters were the guests of honor at an NAACP reception in support of the organization's fourth annual Freedom Fund Dinner. The following March he shared the podium in Sacramento, California, with Governor Pat Brown for an NAACP-sponsored discussion called "The Importance of Civil Rights."

Later that year Cannonball helped stage a benefit to support the Freedom Riders for CORE (the Congress of Racial Equality), an organization founded in 1941 to fight segregation. The Freedom Rides were stimulated by the Supreme Court's ruling on *Boynton v. Virginia* (1960), which declared segregation in interstate bus and rail stations unconstitutional. The Freedom Riders were people—both black and white—who rode public buses throughout the Deep South to test the new law; they were often met with violence and vicious brutality. The June 28 benefit featured the Cannonball Adderley Quintet, Gerry Mulligan, and Louis Armstrong.

In June Cannonball's contract with Riverside was up for renewal. His relationship with the label had been more than just satisfactory; it had rejuvenated his career and made him a star. As part of the agreement, however, Cannonball asked that his Junat Productions control the rights to subsequent recordings he made for the label. This decision would serve him well when he moved on after Riverside's demise three years later.

On July 10 Cannonball created some controversy when he appeared on ABC-TV's *PM East* program, during which he told the host, Mike Wallace, that he could listen to a record and tell the color of a man's skin. Cannonball explained this ability by saying that he was able to distinguish black and white musicians not by their skin color, but by their social patterns. He also said that his goal was to seek dignity for the Negro jazz musician, which he believed had been stereotyped as either a drug addict or a clownish remnant of minstrelsy.

It was also announced that Cannonball had been named by New York's

Mayor Robert F. Wagner Jr. as co-chairman of the mayor's Committee on Narcotics. Throughout his life Adderley was a vocal opponent of drug use. He was especially conscious of the public perception of jazz musicians as being associated with illicit drugs. A November 1960 issue of *Playboy* included a roundtable discussion of the matter that included contributions by Cannonball and Nat Adderley, Dizzy Gillespie, Stan Kenton, Duke Ellington, Billy Taylor, Shelly Manne, Jimmy Giuffre, and Nat Hentoff, the critic for *Down Beat*. Duke Ellington said that playing an instrument was a matter of skill and coordination, and thus a man's best performance would be when he had complete control of his faculties. Cannonball disagreed, saying, "I have played with many musicians who were stoned out of their minds and played like never before." Dizzy Gillespie said that it depended on the degree of genius in the musician.

Most of the panel believed that heavy drug use was no longer "a fad" among jazz musicians, yet Cannonball noted that police would harass jazz musicians (citing Horace Silver, for one) because of the stigma that attached to them from the publicity generated by well-known drug users like Charlie Parker and Billie Holiday. Gillespie pointed out that he was unable to have promoters bill him as the "King of Bebop" because of this attitude.

In the end, Nat Adderley said, half jokingly, that the only solution to drug abuse was to throw everybody—junkies, pushers, and crooks—in jail. "Then we'll all start taking something else, like grass. Then they'll outlaw grass. Nobody will have a lawn!"

Cannonball's vehement aversion to hard drugs was rooted in a harrowing experience from his boyhood. According to his wife, Olga, when he was a teenager performing in the Rabbit's Foot Minstrel Show in the early 1940s another musician offered him some heroin, promising him it would make him play better. Upon injecting it Cannonball became deathly ill; he thereupon vowed never to touch hard drugs again, a promise he honored to his dying day.

In January 1961 Cannonball was hired to write a regular column for the *New York Amsterdam News*, New York City's newspaper for the African American community. The column was called "Cannonball on the Jazz Scene" and included Adderley's musings about jazz performance, fellow musicians he played with, and various aspects of the music business.

IDENTIFICATION CARD

C 24139

Name Julian E. Adderley
Local Address 532 NW 20th Avenue
Employed self-employed (musician)
Description: Age 27 Height 5'9" Weight 240
Eyes mar. Hair blk. Build stocky
This card is to be used for Identification Purposes only
FORT LAUDERDALE POLICE DEPARTMENT
R. R. KELLEY, Chief
Date 2-11-55 By CHAS. E. THISLER
Good for Two Years Ident. Bureau

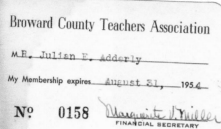

Broward County Teachers Association

Mr. Julian E. Adderly

My Membership expires August 31, 1954

N° 0158 Marguerite S. Miller
FINANCIAL SECRETARY

NATIONAL EDUCATION ASSOCIATION
OF THE UNITED STATES

Signature of Member
1953 1954
is an Active Member of this Association with dues
paid for the year ending August 31, 1954.
W. A. Early William G. Carr
President Executive Secretary
National Headquarters, 1201 Sixteenth St., N. W., Washington 6, D. C.

FSTA Florida State Teachers Association, Inc.
449 W. Georgia St.
Tallahassee, Florida
This is to Certify that
the person named below is a member of the Association

with
dues
paid Mr. Julian Adderly
for the 532 N. W. 2oth Ave.
year Ft. Lauderdale, Fla.
1955

N° 1752 Gilbert L. Porter
Executive Secretary

Julian Adderley, Sr. (1904–1989),
father of Cannonball and Nat
Adderley. Photo courtesy of Olga
Adderley Chandler.

Nat and Julian as children.
Photo courtesy of
Alison Adderley.

24139

Contents of Julian Adderley's wallet, about
the time he made his celebrated debut at
Café Bohemia in New York City. Included
are his identification card and photo, a
Broward County Teachers Association card,
and membership cards for the NEA and
the Florida State Teachers Association.
Courtesy of Olga Adderley Chandler.

Cannonball's first appearance on a record, the Savoy LP *Bohemia After Dark* by the Kenny Clarke Septet, June 1955. The only name mentioned on the front of the album is that of "Cannonball." (*L–R:* Nat Adderley, Donald Byrd, Paul Chambers, Kenny Clarke, Horace Silver, Jerome Richardson, and Cannonball Adderley.) Photo courtesy of John Sellards.

Presenting Julian "Cannonball" Adderley, EmArcy Records, 1955. Cannonball's good-natured exuberance comes across immediately in the cover photo. Photo from the author's collection.

The Miles Davis Sextet, c. 1959. (*L–R:* Bill Evans, Paul Chambers, Miles Davis, John Coltrane, and Cannonball Adderley. Missing from the photo is drummer Jimmy Cobb.) Photo © Ted Williams/CTSIMAGES.

Cannonball waits his turn for a solo, in characteristic pose, fingers snapping, hand rotating with the groove. Photo © Riccardo Schwamenthal/ CTSIMAGES.

The Cannonball Adderley Quintet in San Francisco, the breakthrough album for Cannonball and the soul jazz genre, 1959. Photo from the author's collection.

Riverside Records publicity flyer for its European distributor, Fontana Records, promoting an appearance by the Quintet in the Netherlands. Photo courtesy of Olga Adderley Chandler.

Julian and Nat relax at home in between tours. Photo courtesy of Roy McCurdy.

Cannonball and Nat returned to their alma mater, Florida A&M University annually to play for the school marching band. The Adderleys kept up a busy schedule of concerts and clinics at high schools and colleges across the country. Photo courtesy of Olga Adderley Chandler.

Olga and Julian Adderley, in love, in Italy,
shortly after their 1962 marriage.
Photo courtesy of Olga Adderley Chandler.

Front line of the Cannonball Adderley Sextet, c. 1963.
(*L–R:* Nat Adderley, Cannonball Adderley, and Yusef
Lateef.) Photo courtesy of Olga Adderley Chandler.

Famous Capitol
Records album cover
featuring a sleek
Nancy Wilson and a
svelte Cannonball
Adderley, 1962.
From the author's
collection.

Joe Zawinul, in a pensive mood. Photo © Ray Avery/ CTSIMAGES

The Cannonball Adderley Quintet makes an appearance on French television, c. mid-1960s. Photo courtesy of Olga Adderley Chandler.

"Cannon's Theme," one of two 45-rpm singles recorded at The Club in Chicago. Photo from the author's collection.

Sheet music for the original version of "Mercy, Mercy, Mercy." This was the first of four sets of lyrics for the hit composed by Joe Zawinul. Photo from the author's collection.

Capitol LP of *Mercy, Mercy, Mercy*, recorded at Capitol's Studio A, but promoted as being recorded at The Club in Chicago, 1966. Photo courtesy of John Sellards.

The Cannonball Adderley Quintet, c. 1972. (*L–R:* Roy McCurdy, Walter Booker, George Duke, Nat Adderley, and Cannonball Adderley.) Photo courtesy of Roy McCurdy.

Cannonball Adderley,1974. Photo © Raymond Ross Archives/CTSIMAGES.

Although it was promised that he would write a column every week, his schedule didn't always permit it. He wrote twenty-three columns between January and October of that year before terminating the agreement. Today the columns are invaluable in analyzing Cannonball's thought processes and experiences during this period in his life. At thirty-two, he was in mid-career and at the peak of his popularity. The columns were just like the man himself: thoughtful, witty, analytical, conversational, and articulate.

In his initial column, published on January 21, 1961, he evaluated the differences between the styles and personalities of Miles Davis and Dizzy Gillespie. The next column was a classic, in which Cannonball defined the various degrees of "hipness" among his fans. The most "unhip" person, he wrote, was the "square," one who talks during songs but applauds when they are finished. Serious jazz enthusiasts listen intently and applaud after solos. But Cannonball's favorite fan was what he called "the hippy," a fan who is "very quiet except for occasional utterances such as 'Yeah, baby.' They nod their heads in tempo. They seem to enjoy the music but they applaud only after exceptionally well-played solos and after certain selections are announced. Hippy is a very important cat. Hippy is the cat who'll tell you where it's at." According to Cannonball, "hippy" is the barometer that determines a jazz musician's real level of success and accomplishment.

Other columns paid tribute to well-known jazz figures such as Billy Taylor, Norman Granz, Horace Silver, Duke Ellington, the Heath brothers, Gil Evans, Dave Brubeck, and Quincy Jones. He also often wondered about jazz critics' credibility given that most were not musicians themselves, in one column quoting Horace Silver's query at the renowned jazz symposium at Miles Davis's house: "What qualifications are necessary to become a jazz critic?" In one particularly fascinating column he discussed female vocalists, noting the predominance of such style setters as Ella Fitzgerald, Dinah Washington, Sarah Vaughan, and Billie Holiday, as well as the ability of current singers to succeed "if manager-husbands are avoided"—with his own discovery, Nancy Wilson, heading the list. (Others mentioned included Etta James, Etta Jones, and Aretha Franklin.)

His last column, printed in the October 21 edition of the *News*, was, characteristically, a quiz on jazz, something the former high school music teacher couldn't resist. Readers were challenged to answer questions identifying the leader of the Savoy Sultans (Al Cooper), the trumpet soloist on Duke Ellington's "Take the 'A' Train" (Ray Nance), and the identity of "the Twentieth-Century Gabriel" (Erskine Hawkins).

At the end of January, after concluding a pair of big-band sessions led by bassist Sam Jones, Cannonball recorded the first of three sessions that would result in an "after hours" quartet album (*Know What I Mean*) utilizing the talents of pianist Bill Evans and the Modern Jazz Quartet's Percy Heath and Connie Kay. The sessions were spelled by a big-band session designed specifically to deliver a 45-rpm single for Cannonball. Riverside's Bill Grauer had heard British saxophonist Johnny Dankworth's arrangement of a song called "African Waltz," which Grauer commissioned for Ernie Wilkins to rearrange for Cannonball. The record—probably the first jazz record to feature a piccolo lead (played by Jerome Richardson)—became the first Adderley single to crack *Billboard's* "Hot 100" chart, peaking at no. 41. An ad in *Billboard* excitedly announced that 110,650 copies of the single were shipped on the first day of release. Cannonball Adderley was described in the ad as "the best selling jazz star; big now and getting bigger every minute." "African Waltz" was the first in a series of jazz instrumentals to strike the charts, a pattern that would continue throughout the decade thanks to artists such as Ramsey Lewis ("The In Crowd"), Jimmy Smith ("Walk on the Wild Side"), and Vince Guaraldi ("Cast Your Fate to the Wind"). Keepnews followed up by issuing an album featuring "African Waltz" as its centerpiece.

Cannonball's popularity was now expanding to more commercial enterprises. In February, he recorded three one-minute music tracks for television commercials advertising Prell shampoo. The session was most likely one of the first jazz tracks ever used for a TV commercial.

Two days after the *African Waltz* big-band album was completed, the Cannonball Adderley Quintet was back in the studio to record one of their most satisfying albums, *The Cannonball Adderley Quintet Plus*. The "plus" in the title referred to pianist Wynton Kelly, who was used on four of the sides, while Victor Feldman was switched to vibraphone. Feldman had left the band after its second European tour concluded at the end of April, so Cannonball was once again on the hunt for another pianist. Technically speaking, both Kelly and Feldman could be considered the "Plus" in the album title, since at the time neither was a regular member of the Quintet. Kelly was featured on one of his typically bluesy compositions, "Winetone," an improvised jam that took its name from the Chicago disc jockey "Daddy-O" Daylie's exaggerated pronunciation of Kelly's first name.

After the session, Cannonball used Walter Bishop on piano for a two-week date in Washington, D.C., but he didn't find a permanent replacement until the end of June. Meanwhile he and Nat formed their own production company, which they called Junat, for which they intended to produce records, concerts, and television pilots.

Cannonball had been producing sessions for Riverside since 1960, which resulted in over a dozen LPs by Budd Johnson, Clifford Jordan, Sam Jones, and others. One of the sessions was by a Washington-based jazz quintet that included Andrew White, alto sax; Ray Codrington, trumpet; Harry Killgo, piano; Walter Booker Jr., bass; and Carl Newman, drums. The group was dubbed the JFK Quintet, as a tribute to President Kennedy's ideology of change and new ideas. Two LPs were issued by Riverside, but the band did not last. Booker, however, became a member of Adderley's Quintet in 1969.

Before leaving the band, Victor Feldman participated in a round-robin interview with the members of the Quintet that was published as a two-part series in *Down Beat*. In the article, titled "Inside the Cannonball Adderley Quintet," the band members discussed reverse discrimination, which they referred to as "Crow Jim," in which white jazz musicians such as Feldman and Bill Evans were thought to be not as "authentic" in their playing as their African American counterparts. All of the musicians agreed that the key to jazz performance was that there had to be a pulse to generate momentum, and that a good, solid rhythm section was necessary as the source of that propulsive energy.

Ever since Cannonball Adderley started his Quintet in 1955, he had been searching for a pianist who would complete the jigsaw puzzle of sound that he wished to create. Up until 1961 the other three positions in his Quintet—Nat Adderley on cornet, Sam Jones on bass, and Louis Hayes on drums—had been a stabilizing force, but the pianist's position had been a revolving door, with Hank Jones, Bill Evans, Bobby Timmons, Wynton Kelly, Junior Mance, Barry Harris, Victor Feldman, and Walter

Bishop all serving time in the band. In June 1961 Cannonball finally found a pianist who not only fit the musical sound he was trying to create, but also would stay with him for the next nine and a half years.

11

ONSKA

Josef Zawinul was born in Vienna, Austria, on July 7, 1932. A gifted child, Zawinul was singled out by the Nazi government for his innate musical ability, and at the age of seven he was enrolled in the Vienna Conservatory as a classical piano student. The family managed to survive the endless Allied forces' bombings, and after the war Josef, because of his talent, was one of a few dozen students who were transferred from their homes to the Czech Sudetenland. There he lived in a huge estate that dated back to the days of the monarchy.

He fell in love with American musical culture by listening to radio programs, which inspired him to play jazz. (The first jazz tune he learned was Fats Waller's "Honeysuckle Rose.") In 1951 or 1952 a friend of Zawinul's, a concert pianist named Friedrich Gulder, visited New York and brought back records by Charlie Parker, Dizzy Gillespie, and Duke Ellington. These recordings spurred Zawinul to begin trying to play jazz himself.

In 1958, after seeing an ad in *Down Beat* magazine, Zawinul applied for and received a scholarship to attend the Berklee School of Music in Boston. He arrived in the United States in 1959 but spent only three days at Berklee before ditching the college and hunting down jazz jobs in New York nightclubs. In later interviews, he explained that he had used the scholarship in order to get entrance to the United States.

Within three weeks after hopping off the boat, he was discovered by trumpeter Maynard Ferguson, who hired the young pianist to play in his big band, replacing Bob Dogan, who was about to ship out for his army service. Zawinul's tenure with the Ferguson band only lasted a few months; he was let go for "insubordination," ostensibly because Ferguson feared that Zawinul was trying to take over the band.

From there Zawinul went to work for vocalist Dinah Washington, playing blues piano in her group for the next nineteen months. Many musicians were surprised at how adept at the blues Zawinul was, especially when they found out about his background. After Washington, he worked with singer Joe Williams and trumpeter Harry "Sweets" Edison before joining Cannonball Adderley in April 1961.

When Cannonball started searching for a pianist to replace Victor Feldman, he was delighted to discover that Zawinul played blues in a style reminiscent of Bobby Timmons. The revolving door that was the piano chair in the Cannonball Adderley Quintet, which hadn't been able to keep the position filled for more than a few months at a time, had nothing to do with politics or with the reputation pianists had as being a restless sort. It was chiefly a matter of coincidence. When Cannonball started his second Quintet, he more or less stole Timmons from Art Blakey. But Timmons felt guilty about leaving, especially since his composition "Moanin'" had become such a huge hit for Blakey's Jazz Messengers. Barry Harris replaced Timmons when "Dis Here" was being demanded by patrons everywhere, but after a while Harris got fed up with having to play his predecessor's composition so often. Victor Feldman left because his new wife did not want him to go out on the road, fearing the carnal enticements musicians often encounter in that lifestyle. When Joe Zawinul was hired to replace Feldman, Cannonball finally achieved the stability, in terms of personnel as well as musically, that he had been seeking. From the very start, Zawinul fit into the Adderley scheme of things like a glove. His playing proved once and for all that white musicians could have just as much soul as black ones.

Soon after Zawinul joined, the band went into the recording studio, but not for Riverside Records. Instead, they were brought in to accompany another Adderley discovery, the twenty-four-year-old singer Nancy Wilson, whom Cannonball had been mentoring since 1959. Wilson began displaying her abilities as a singer at the age of four, when she started singing in church choirs in her hometown of Chillicothe, Ohio, and imitating singers she had heard on the radio. At the age of fifteen she won a talent contest on a local television station; she was singing at clubs while she was still in high school.

After a year at college, where she studied to be a teacher, Wilson left school to join Rusty Bryant's big band, touring with the group throughout Canada and the Midwest from 1956 to 1958. After arriving in New York in 1959, she filled in for singer Irene Reid at a Bronx nightclub called the Blue Morocco, where Cannonball Adderley first heard her perform. Impressed, he introduced her to his manager, John Levy, who negotiated a regular gig for her at the Blue Morocco and also secured a recording deal with Capitol Records. Her first album, *Like in Love*, was issued later that year, with an orchestra led by Capitol's stalwart bandleader and arranger Billy May. That album, and the four that followed, stressed Wilson's rhythm-and-blues and pop tendencies, but on her second release she also had the benefit of the accompaniment of Ben Webster's rich tenor sax. In 1961 Levy arranged for Cannonball to produce her next Capitol album under the aegis of his and Nat's new Junat Productions. The result was what many view as the masterpiece of Nancy Wilson's recording career.

On June 27 and 29, 1961, Wilson and Cannonball Adderley's Quintet recorded six songs together, which would constitute one side of the LP. The B side consisted of instrumentals by the Quintet, recorded during a two-day session in August. Wilson's selections mixed jazz pieces with contemporary show tunes, including "Never Will I Marry" (from *Greenwillow*, a flop musical by Frank Loesser), a ballad that was transformed into an uptempo swinger, and "Happy Talk," from Rodgers and Hammerstein's *South Pacific*, which also kicked up its heels. "The Old Country" was one of the best, a Nat Adderley--Curtis Lewis collaboration with a medium swing and a melancholy melody that featured a rich solo by Cannonball.

Nancy Wilson's vocal style was hugely influenced by Little Jimmy Scott, the "Grandfather of Soul." By listening to Scott, Wilson developed a highly emotional, yet unsentimental style that helped blaze a trail for other jazz-influenced pop singers of the 1960s. It was no accident that one of the first numbers she sang on the first day of the session was Scott's "The Masquerade Is Over," on which the Adderleys laid out, leaving Zawinul's sophisticated piano, Sam Jones's bass, and Louis Hayes's brushes to complete the wistful mood set by Wilson's vocal.

Although Joe Zawinul had few opportunities to stretch out during the vocal session, this would change when it came time for the Quintet to record the instrumental titles for the B side of the record. On August 23 the band recorded a number that would become the group's theme song, played to open and close most of their concerts during the 1960s: "Unit Seven" (otherwise known as "Cannon's Theme"), written by bassist Sam Jones, featured a hurricane-force saxophone solo from Cannonball. Zawinul followed Nat's cornet solo with one of his own that showed his predilection for the blues. One of the album's other highlights was a gorgeous rendition of "I Can't Get Started," the Vernon Duke--Ira Gershwin show tune made famous by trumpeter Bunny Berigan. Sandwiching Cannonball's two luxurious solos, Zawinul played a beautifully restrained melodic interlude of his own.

The cover of the LP, simply titled *Nancy Wilson/Cannonball Adderley*, became famous in its own right: it showed a sleek Nancy Wilson, in a form-fitting orange dress, standing beside a svelte-looking Cannonball against a stark white background. The album became the first one by Wilson to make the best-selling album charts in *Billboard*, although she was never known for being a chart-topping artist. The album was a great success not just for Wilson, but for Capitol Records as well, although today many fans wish that Wilson and the Adderleys had performed together on the entire album instead of just one side. (Less than three years later Cannonball Adderley would also join the roster of Capitol Records.)

In the late summer of 1961, while in Kansas City enjoying some rare time off, Cannonball Adderley ran into an old idol, blues singer Eddie "Cleanhead" Vinson. Cannonball used to listen to Vinson's alto saxophone solos in the 1940s, when Cleanhead was playing with Cootie Williams's big band. Adderley later recalled that it was some time before he even knew Vinson's full name; he was always announced on the radio as "Mr. Cleanhead." Now Adderley was riding high, and Vinson had all but been forgotten in the heady days of hard bop and early soul. Part of Cannonball's agreement with Riverside Records was that he had a free hand to record anyone he felt was deserving, and during an engagement at the Birdhouse in Chicago he set up a recording session for the Quintet to back Vinson on an album of blues.

The one-day session resulted in six tracks being issued on Vinson's

Riverside album *Back Door Blues*. Although the blues was Cannonball's favorite musical environment, he resisted the temptation to play saxophone on the album except for the songs on which Vinson sang, graciously deferring to his idol and happy to remain in the background as producer. Two of Vinson's songs, "Back Door Blues" and "Hold It!," were issued on a 45-rpm single. The single was doing particularly well in Chicago until its momentum was killed by a local preacher, who attacked the immorality of the lyrics to "Back Door Blues" (about a man's affair with a married woman). After the single started to take off, Cannonball ushered Vinson and the Quintet back into the studio on Valentine's Day, 1962, to record four more vocal numbers. In 1988 Orrin Keepnews added another three tracks from the first session to an LP reissue called *Cleanhead and Cannonball*.

On November 25 the Quintet was one of the featured acts at the African Carnival, a three-day celebration of arts of Africa and the African diaspora sponsored by the African Research Foundation and held at the Sixty-ninth Regiment Armory in New York. The eclectic program featured an array of performers that included percussionists Michael Olatunji (Nigeria) and Mongo Santamaría (Cuba) and Haitian dancer and choreographer Jean-Léon Destiné; they alternated with such American performers as Oscar Brown Jr., comedian Dick Gregory, and singers Diahann Carroll and Johnny Nash. The show also featured sixty dancers and displays of African arts and crafts in a setting meant to replicate an "authentic African village." Although this show was but one of many weekend festivals in which Adderley participated during his career, it is notable because it marked his first public acknowledgment of the African roots of jazz, soul, and other styles. Later in his career he would celebrate this connection vividly by wearing vibrantly colored traditional African dashikis during performances instead of the staid dark suits customary in his earlier shows.

After returning from a trip to Paris, where he supervised recordings by Kenny Clarke and Bud Powell, Cannonball began 1962 by adding the avant-garde musician Yusef Lateef to his group. He had considered expanding to a sextet in September 1961, wishing to add a third voice to the front line of himself and Nat. The idea was to create a more effective background/accompaniment for whoever was playing a solo. His search for a versatile person to complete the front line initially targeted the trombonist Curtis Fuller, but Fuller decided to sign with Art Blakey. According to Lateef, it was John Levy who convinced Cannonball to hire him.

Born in Chattanooga, Tennessee, on October 9, 1920, William Emanuel Huddleston changed his name to Yusef Lateef in 1950 when he converted to the Ahmadiyya sect of Islam. When he was five his family moved to Detroit, where he grew up. During his formative years Lateef came into contact with other Detroit-based musicians who would become well-known in the jazz field, including Kenny Burrell, Milt Jackson, Paul Chambers, and Elvin Jones.

Although initially a tenor saxophonist, Lateef learned to play other reed instruments as well, including the oboe, an instrument not normally associated with jazz. In 1949 he toured briefly with Dizzy Gillespie before returning to Detroit to attend college at Wayne State University, where he studied composition and learned to play flute, an instrument that had been used sparingly in jazz up to that time owing to its lack of volume and its being perceived as a "feminine"-sounding instrument. His teacher was Larry Teal, a flutist with the Detroit Symphony who also played alto saxophone solos. Teal would become a renowned saxophone teacher until his retirement in 1974 and had a huge influence on Lateef's playing, on both flute and saxophone.

In the late 1940s and early '50s the use of the flute in Afro-Cuban jazz helped influence greater use of the instrument in jazz. Most, like Lateef, started out as reedmen, adopting the flute as just another instrument in their arsenal. But one player, Herbie Mann, specialized in flute and revolutionized its use in jazz. The flute enabled Lateef, like Mann, to explore world music styles, since most cultures featured some kind of flutelike instrument in their traditional makeup.

Lateef made his first record as a leader for Savoy in 1957, in addition to also recording for Prestige. In 1961 his albums *Into Something* and *Eastern Sounds* showcased his interest in music from India and the Far East, as he performed on such exotic instruments as the Chinese globular flute (also known as the xun). His musical adventurousness was not, however, translating into a lucrative living, so his manager, John Levy, introduced him to his own most successful client, Cannonball Adderley.

Cannonball was excited at the prospect of exploring world music avenues with an accomplished musician like Lateef in his group. He was eager for Lateef to play not only saxophone, but a closetful of other instruments, including a variety of handmade native flutes. All of this gave Cannonball a variety of musical colors with which to work. His presence even inspired Cannonball to pick up the flute again himself, which he had discarded when he began his jazz career, although Lateef says he never saw Cannonball play the instrument. With the versatile Lateef on board, suddenly all kinds of options were available to Cannonball. Lateef even started learning the bass, freeing up Sam Jones to play more songs on the cello.

Lateef became friends with everyone in the group, but he had a special relationship with Joe Zawinul. "Joe and I developed a little language like Lester Young had," Lateef remembered. "One word I remembered was 'onska,' which meant 'that's all right.'" Lateef became known for utilizing unusual techniques in his flute playing. Although some attribute the ability to hum and play flute simultaneously to Sam Most, Lateef believes that the technique had been used in Cuba a century before Most started doing it in the 1950s.

Fifty years later Lateef still bristles at being called a jazz musician. "I've never played jazz. That's an ambiguous term. Improvisation is a funny word. As I understand it, improvisation means to do something without previous preparation. That's not the case in learning to play the flute. It's the outcome of your years of training and study that enables you to play spontaneously when given a set of chord changes."

Cannonball kept in mind that in order to earn a living, experimentation, especially at live dates, had to be set aside in favor of what the audiences wanted to hear. He drew an especially hard line when it came to longer works, such as the Modern Jazz Quartet's "Fontessa." In a June 1962 interview in *Down Beat*, Cannonball said, "I will not go into a night club and play extended compositions. It just doesn't make sense. I think it is impractical for jazz in general and us in particular. It would actually lose customers for jazz."

The live session occurred during a weeklong engagement at the Village Vanguard, during which the newly christened Cannonball Adderley Sextet made its first recordings. After the success of the first two live albums at the Jazz Workshop in San Francisco and the Lighthouse in Hermosa Beach,

Orrin Keepnews decided that the time was right to record an album at a live setting in New York and chose an engagement at the Village Vanguard on January 12 and 14. Keepnews and Cannonball had been reticent about recording in New York because California audiences were looser and more responsive to the group than New York's more reserved patrons—something Cannonball was only too glad to point out to the Village Vanguard audience in his typically erudite introduction to the group's set at the matinee concert on Friday, January 12.

> You know, you get a lot of people who are supposed to be hip, and they act like they're supposed to be hip, which makes a big difference. Now we have especially been impressed with the audience here at the matinee performance at the Village Vanguard. We think that this is the kind of audience that is the "real" jazz audience. And we want to thank you for making it possible for being so really hip. Hipness is not a state of mind, it's a fact of life. You don't decide you're hip. It just happens that way.

Cannonball then went on to introduce Jimmy Heath's composition "Gemini" by explaining that it had a "schizophrenic" feeling to it. The number, which, like "Dis Here," was in 3/4 time, began with Lateef playing the theme on flute. The crowd responded immediately, yelling out encouragement to Cannonball during his furious opening solo. Nat started his cornet solo more quietly but then it too increased in intensity; he was followed by Lateef, whose tenor solo featured him playing two notes at once, an effect Coltrane had adopted in the 1950s. Following this was a driving three-voice interlude that showcased what Cannonball had envisioned when he added Lateef. Zawinul's blues-oriented piano solo attracted shouts of enthusiasm from the other musicians before Lateef returned to restate the melody on flute.

Lateef contributed two songs to *The Cannonball Adderley Sextet in New York*. One of these, the dirgelike "Syn-Anthesia," was a departure for the Quintet. It was the first time they had ventured into the avant-garde and featured Lateef playing an Eastern-influenced solo on the oboe and some oddly dissonant but captivating three-voice chords. Also of note on this indispensable album was one of Joe Zawinul's first recorded compositions,

"Scotch and Water," "named," as Cannonball blithely observed, for "a subject that he is [an] expert [on]."

Cannonball was not as busy with his musical activities in the first half of 1962 as in previous years. A week after the Village Vanguard session he made a guest appearance on a Ray Brown big-band album for Verve that featured an explosive version of "Work Song." In May he played on a session for Jazzland Records headed by Nat and featuring Ellis Marsalis (father of Wynton and Branford) on piano. In June he spent three days recording as part of a big band headed by Oscar Peterson (with Cannonball and Nat appearing as "Jud and Pat Brotherly"). It was also in June that Cannonball made the most important personnel decision of his life. This addition, however, wasn't a musical one.

12

OLGA

Olga James, who would become Mrs. Julian Adderley, was born in 1930 in Washington, D.C., the daughter of show-business parents. Her father was a saxophonist and her mother a dancer on the "Chitlin' Circuit," a collective name given to venues that hosted entertainment for African American audiences. Olga never knew her father; her parents separated when she was a child, and her mother remarried when Olga was thirteen. Olga's grandparents raised her until she began attending college at Juilliard in New York, at which time she lived with her mother in nearby Newark, New Jersey.

Olga's grandmother always loved listening to the singing of the soprano Ernestine Schumann-Heink, which was one factor in Olga's desire to become a singer herself. The other, more compelling reason was an innate need for attention, perhaps a result of having come from a broken home. At Juilliard she shared a studio with the future opera legend Leontyne Price, where both trained as opera singers, although Olga never really thought she had the proper voice for opera. Instead, she sang Mozart art songs, German lieder, and French chansons. Reflecting on her time at Juilliard, Olga believes that she could have taken better advantage of her education had she been older (she was seventeen when she started her studies). Raising money for tuition was difficult, but Olga was helped out by members of her family, who chipped in enough to get her through school. During the summers she worked; one job was at a factory in New Jersey, where she assembled filaments for light bulbs.

Through her connections at Juilliard she was able to get her first professional job, as a member of the company for a State Department--funded production of Virgil Thomson's opera *Four Saints in Three Acts*, which was performed at a festival in Paris. After she returned to New York, she didn't work for an entire year, but through an aunt she landed a job in Atlantic City's Club Harlem with the black revue *Larry Steele's Smart Affairs*. When the revue traveled to Chicago, a woman who had auditioned all of the Juilliard students remembered the petite, vivacious young actress and sent her to audition for Otto Preminger's film adaptation of *Carmen Jones*, an all-black musical based on Georges Bizet's opera *Carmen*. Olga played Cindy Lou (the Micaela character), the fiancée of Joe, played by Harry Belafonte (as the Don José character).

In 1956 Olga appeared opposite Sammy Davis Jr. as the ingenue Ethel Pearson in *Mr. Wonderful*, a Broadway musical that served as a showcase for Davis's nightclub act. The show ran for nearly a year, closing in February 1957 after 383 performances. During her time with the show, Olga became friends with Miles Davis's wife, Frances, who sang in the ensemble. One evening in 1956 Frances took Olga to see Miles's group perform at a nightclub. Cannonball happened to be sitting in on this particular night, and Frances introduced him to Olga. The saxophonist was gracious and elegant when he came over to the ladies' table to say hello. Olga later remembered being attracted during that meeting by Cannonball's sense of humor.

The next time they saw each other was four years later in Los Angeles. Olga had her own nightclub act by then and was about to embark on a tour to Australia and the Philippines. Cannonball was playing at the Mocambo with Nancy Wilson and remembered meeting Olga from his gig with Miles Davis. When he came over to greet her, Olga was struck by how handsome Cannonball looked in his tuxedo.

In March 1962 Olga agreed to go with her friend Jo Basile King to Birdland to see Adderley's Quintet perform again. She was tired from touring and didn't want to go, but Jo insisted. Before beginning his set, Cannonball saw her in the audience, came over to her table, sat down, and stunned Olga by telling her that one day she would be his wife. They both laughed over that, but soon afterward they started dating. They quickly fell in love and began making plans to marry.

It was a brief engagement. On June 28 Julian Adderley and Olga James were married at New York City Hall. Although Cannonball was a star, the event was not publicized until after the fact, and the ceremony, performed by the city clerk (Olga recalled that although Cannonball was raised in a churchgoing household, he was not religious, and she never knew him to attend church), took place "without pomp or flair." The best man was Lee Weaver, a friend of Cannonball's from Florida who would later co-star with Olga as Bill Cosby's brother and sister-in-law, Brian and Verna Kincaid, on *The Bill Cosby Show* (1969–70). A small reception was held at the New Yorker Hotel, with friends, family, and their managers in attendance. The newlyweds then got on a train and headed down to Florida, where they were met by Cannonball's parents, who immediately whisked them to the Episcopal church where he and Nat had served as altar boys when they were growing up. Although Cannonball thought that they were being taken there just to be blessed by the minister, in fact the Adderleys had arranged for a proper church wedding there. Without it there was no way that Mrs. Adderley would let Julian and Olga sleep together in her house. The couple spent the next week honeymooning in Miami Beach at the Fontainebleau Hotel. When they returned to Tallahassee, they were guests of honor at a garden party arranged by Cannonball's parents. Some two hundred people attended the event, which was held on his parents' lawn.

Other than his brother Nat, nobody knew Cannonball Adderley better than Olga. They had a happy life together and remained devoted to one another until his death in 1975. Olga's insights into Cannonball's personality have proved valuable in shedding light on his life out of the limelight.

> We decided to get married in June because I was doing stock and he was on the road all the time, and I think if we hadn't married then, that it would have been pretty hard for our relationship to stick. After we got married, Miles offered us an apartment in his townhouse. We lived way out in Queens and Julian did not want to live in town, and as much as he admired Miles, he did not want to be part of that scene. He said he did not want people dropping in on him the way they dropped in on Miles.

Julian was a basic country boy. Stanley Crouch called him a "sophisticated country boy" and I think that was a very apt description. In addition to having eclectic tastes in music, he also had very fine taste in other things, and a wide range of interests. He was very intelligent and funny, but not only was he interesting, he was interested. At base, his values were country values, despite all the other things that musicians do, in terms of how he wanted his home life to be and his life to be. That was at base who he was. He was very close to his parents, who were both teachers. He especially admired his father.

One of the things that I found really attractive about him and one of the reasons I married him was because I didn't have a father and it influenced my life. I admired all of those responsible men like Julian's father, his brother, Julian himself, and the men in his band. If you think about it, most of the men in his band were college educated, and all of them came from intact families. People don't think that about jazz musicians. If there's a stereotype about jazz musicians, they were not it. They were not "good boys" all the time, but they were all responsible men.

Julian taught me jazz. It was a beautiful period in our lives because he played records by his favorite performers for me and explained things and it was a beautiful introduction to jazz.

He belonged to a group and the group all had input, even though he was the leader. Their chemistry was the important thing, and you have to understand that, initially, I didn't know anything about jazz other than what he taught me. The only thing that I think I may have influenced him on was doing the *Fiddler on the Roof* album, because Jerry Bock wrote music for that show as well as for *Mr. Wonderful*. Julian had very eclectic taste. He liked show tunes, he liked classical music, he liked everything.

Julian and Nat were very close. Although it was Julian's band, they had big fights about various things. If you talk to Orrin Keepnews, he will tell you that every time they made a recording, they had a big argument, but it never meant that they were not close and it didn't mean that they didn't love each other. Nat wanted the band to be called the Adderley Brothers but it was Julian's band. He was the dominant one and I understand that he was a very good leader. People said that he developed the musicians in his band.

When Julian was in Miles's band, evidently he had a stroke of some kind. He didn't expect to live past forty. When he finally turned forty, I gave him a surprise birthday party in San Francisco, and he really was surprised. His whole family had diabetes, except for his father. Julian's weight certainly had a lot to do with his diabetes. He never seriously tried losing weight but would go on minor diets and lose ten pounds. But then he'd get away from me and go out on the road and I'd find candy bars in his suitcase when he came home. He was really very bad about losing weight and about his diet. But because of that stroke and because he had a very short lifeline in his hand, he never felt he was going to live a long life, and I think that probably his thinking was, "Why should I be careful? I'm going to die young anyhow."

He loved to eat. He made a mean gumbo. Julian was a very good cook; he even taught me to cook. When we got married, I figured out how to scramble eggs and do steak, but he was really sweet about that because when I learned to cook something, I'd get stuck on it and he'd be very nice about eating it day after day until finally he'd say, "You know what? I really don't like this every day." He was a sweet man and a nice man. He was intelligent, had a wide range of interests, and he was good to me. Yes he was.

13

THE CANNONBALL EXPRESS

In October 1962 Cannonball Adderley received the honor of becoming the first entertainer ever to have a train named after him when the Long Island Railroad named their New York–to–Montauk run "the Cannonball Express." The all-parlor-car train was the only one in the nation with an open-end observation car. This was but one of many honors received by Cannonball in the wake of his successful Riverside albums and nonstop concert touring.

The Sextet's touring schedule was becoming more complicated—European venues were vying with one another to entice him to bring his group abroad. Between the summer of 1962 and the end of 1963 the band played the Belgium Jazz Festival; completed a European tour of Sweden, Italy, and Switzerland; and embarked on their first tour of Japan.

In September 1962 the Sextet made a return appearance to the Jazz Workshop in San Francisco, where Orrin Keepnews recorded on parts of three days of the three-week engagement. This session is noted for the debut of another Adderley crowd-pleaser, "The Jive Samba." Written by Nat Adderley, the song had already been recorded during a March 1962 appearance at Birdland, but the Jazz Workshop version was the first to be released.

The LP, titled *Jazz Workshop Revisited*, also featured a song that Cannonball loved introducing. In his hip, florid introduction to "Primitivo," Cannonball explained:

The tune sounds pretty much as the name implies. It is very primitive, loose, sometimes disjointed, but very colorful. It's got a lot of primitive rhythms and primitive harmonies, but rich rhythms and rich harmonies. So, in this case, we'd like to have you understand what we are trying to convey and we hope we can reach you, the base and primitive elements in you.

The song featured Lateef starting off with an exotic sounding solo on a bamboo flute that he had built, accompanied by Sam Jones on cello. This was followed by Cannonball's alto solo, which was punctuated by high-register shrieks from Nat's cornet. Lateef took another mystical solo on oboe in a middle section that brought to mind some of Eric Dolphy's work on John Coltrane's *Africa/Brass* from 1961. (In his introduction to the Birdland performance of the number, Cannonball warned the audience, which was used to hearing straight-ahead numbers like "Work Song" and "Dis Here," by saying, "Don't be alarmed! Be cool!")

In addition to embracing world music, brought to his attention by Lateef, Cannonball Adderley also shared his love and knowledge of classical music with his bandmates. "At various times he would talk about Stravinsky and different symphonic composers," Lateef said. "He was very much informed about Western music, everyone from Respighi to Wagner. When you listen to him, it is obvious that he was well trained. You can hear it in what he played. I introduced him to ragas and other Indian forms as well as twelve-tone music."

While in San Francisco the Sextet (minus Lateef) recorded a television show in the *Jazz Casual* series, a program produced by Ralph Gleason and Dick Christian that sought to educate the public on the background and rich history of jazz. The segment featuring the Quintet focused on the blues. Each of their three songs, "Scotch and Water," "Arriving Soon," and "Unit 7," was prefaced by Cannonball's articulate explanations of how it fit into the developing blues tradition.

The 1959 film *Black Orpheus* took the jazz world by storm, introducing the music of Brazil's Carnival, the bossa nova, and its more agitated cousin, the samba, to American jazz. The intoxicating melodies and rhythms arrived on the jazz scene in 1962, and the bossa nova became America's newest musical craze. Brazilian music wasn't new to jazz; it had been recorded since the mid-1950s by such artists as Laurindo Almeida and Bud Shank, but up until 1962 only American musicians were used, feeling their way along by trying to copy the intricate Brazilian rhythms.

Flutist Herbie Mann was the first major American jazz musician to want to go to the source to record with musicians who were actually playing and living the music. He told his manager, Monte Kay, that if he wasn't permitted to go to Brazil, he would "commit musical suicide." Once there Mann began to study the most popular bands in Rio de Janeiro, and in October he made a record with the best band Brazil had to offer, Sergio Mendes and his Bossa Rio Sextet.

Two months later Mendes and his band came to New York, where they participated in a session with Cannonball Adderley, minus his Sextet. The album, titled *Cannonball's Bossa Nova*, consisted not of bossa nova versions of Cannonball's hits, nor even his own pseudo-Brazilian "Jive Samba"; instead, the works were authentic, original tunes by some of Brazil's finest songwriters: Antônio Carlos Jobim, João Donato, Maurício Einhorn, and Mendes's guitarist, Durval Ferreira. Cannonball's genius for lyrical playing fit into the bossa nova formula perfectly, and the album displayed an entirely different side of his musicianship, which had previously concentrated on soul jazz and hard bop. Mendes would enjoy a long career in American jazz; he recorded a series of albums with his group before he was signed to Herb Alpert's A&M label, where he enjoyed his greatest commercial success.

In January 1963 *Down Beat* announced that Cannonball Adderley and his Sextet would make appearances at twelve Midwestern universities in a series of lectures combined with performances to help educate students about the history of jazz in America. Cannonball would deliver his lecture and then, on the following day, the Sextet would appear in concert. The first schools mentioned in the tour were Purdue, Notre Dame, Ohio State, and Michigan. But the tour had to be postponed when Cannonball had a serious and mysterious health scare. Olga Adderley recalled:

After we were married about a year, he had a nervous breakdown. He was under a lot of stress because of the touring and had been having trouble with his teeth and his embouchure. We were in Philadelphia and apparently he and Nat were opening at this club and had an argument and some people called me and said that Julian was crying and couldn't stop. So I came over to the club and one of their boyhood friends, Lee Weaver, was there. Lee and I put Julian in a car and drove from Philadelphia to Washington to see his friend, Dr. LaSalle Leffall, an accomplished physician who later became the head of Freedmen's Hospital. [Adderley attended school with Leffall at Florida A&M—at the time, he was an assistant professor of surgery.] From there, we took Julian home to our apartment in New York. He was out of it for quite a while and I had to beg Dr. Leffall not to put him into an institution. While he was asleep I called my internist, who taught at NYU, Dr. Herbert Chasis. He told me to bring Julian in to see him. Julian had consulted a doctor who was in the same building and Dr. Chasis obtained his records, so that's how I found out that he had had a minor stroke. He went to see a psychologist and finally got over it.

Cannonball did not perform again until February 11, when the Sextet played a concert in Atlanta before returning to play Birdland in New York. Next, they played three weeks at the Sutherland Lounge in Chicago and then embarked on a European tour, playing concerts in Sweden, West Germany, at the San Remo Jazz Festival in Italy, and finishing up in Lugano, Switzerland. The highlight of their travels in 1963 was their first tour to Japan, a country with a huge jazz following. A series of concerts was recorded there and one LP was issued, *Nippon Soul*. It would prove to be Cannonball's last record for Riverside.

The 1960s was a time of rapid changes. In November 1963 the Sextet was playing at the Jazz Workshop in San Francisco when they heard about the assassination of President John F. Kennedy. Unlike other entertainment venues across the country, the club—and Adderley—decided not to cancel the concert. "It was very touching," Yusef Lateef recalled. "We all played that night and carried on the best we could. That was our job."

Lateef's contract with the band ended during the San Francisco engagement, and he decided the time was right to leave the Cannonball Adderley Sextet and strike out on his own. The two years Lateef spent with Adderley had resulted in some of the most exceptional and innovative recordings of both their careers. Of his time with Cannonball, Lateef said:

I learned to use my time intelligently. He gave me the opportunity to look into things that ordinarily I would not be in the position to do. I felt that I had discovered what I wanted to find out during those two years, so it was time to go try some of these things out. Two months after I left the group, I was playing at a place called Slug's in New York, and Cannonball came down one night and sat in with the group and he played "The Masquerade Is Over." He played very beautifully that night and it reminded me of those two wonderful years that we played together. . . . I was looking at that time to try and find my own voice. That's what Eric Dolphy told me I should do, instead of copying others. John Coltrane, a good friend and companion, also told me this. Cannonball helped me by giving me a job so I could remain active and give me a chance to write a book on scales. I would not have been able to do this had I not been working. All this time, I studied.

Lateef's last performance with the group took place on January 4, 1964, at McCormick Place in Chicago. He was replaced by the twenty-five-year-old Charles Lloyd, a tenor saxophonist who played in the edgy style being developed by such musicians as Ornette Coleman, Don Cherry, and John Coltrane.

In December 1963 the owner of Riverside Records, Bill Grauer, died unexpectedly of a sudden heart attack; he was only forty years old. It wasn't long before Riverside began going downhill, and finally Orrin Keepnews had to file for bankruptcy. One of the label's creditors was Cannonball Adderley, its most successful artist, who was owed some $7,000. In order to help Keepnews survive, Cannonball offered to extend his contract, but Keepnews refused, telling Cannonball he would be better off signing with another label. Cannonball never pressed Keepnews for the money that was owed him and ended up writing it off as a loss. The Sextet recorded one last session in March 1964 for old time's sake, but the tapes were lost. They have never been issued.

As part of the agreement between Cannonball and Riverside in June 1961, Cannonball retained the rights to albums produced under the name of Junat Productions. These served him well in later years. With the end of Riverside, Cannonball and Nat had to decide what label to go to next.

Little did they know that the label they would end up signing with would represent the apex of the most explosive event in pop music history, when a quartet of mop-topped musicians from Liverpool, England, arrived in New York City to appear on *The Ed Sullivan Show*.

14

AN ASSAULT ON THE TYRANNY OF STYLE

The company that Cannonball Adderley signed with in the summer of 1964 was about as dissimilar to Riverside Records as an entity could get. Capitol Records was one of the giants in the industry. It was started in 1942 by three show-business moguls: songwriter–turned–film producer B. G. "Buddy" DeSylva, lyricist Johnny Mercer, and record-store owner Glenn Wallichs. With Mercer leading the way as a recording artist, Capitol took advantage of its Los Angeles headquarters to sign many top Holly-wood-based music and radio performers to contracts, including Margaret Whiting, Jo Stafford, Paul Whiteman, and Nat "King" Cole. It wasn't long before Capitol drew even with RCA Victor, Columbia, and Decca, joining its rivals to make up the "Big Four" of the record industry.

By the early 1960s Capitol was well established in a variety of musi-cal genres: motion-picture soundtracks, country, light instrumentals, folk, and especially pop and rock music. In 1962 they signed the Beach Boys, a group that would become America's most popular rock band, but the sunny, surf-oriented harmonies of the California quintet was no match for what would come in late 1963, when the label optioned the rights to issue records in the United States by the Beatles.

The one genre in which Capitol was noticeably weak was jazz. In its two decades, Capitol had signed some impressive performers in the field of jazz (chiefly due to the efforts of A&R man Dave Dexter Jr.)—among them Benny Goodman, Art Tatum, Stan Kenton, Louis Prima, George Shearing, and Gerry Mulligan—but had been unable to sustain staying up to date with the current trends in jazz. Capitol's chief claim to fame in the jazz world was its decision to record the young Miles Davis in 1949 and 1950 in sessions that were later marketed as "the Birth of the Cool." But Davis soon moved on to Prestige and finally Columbia, with whom he achieved his greatest success and influence. By 1964 Capitol's jazz roster had been reduced to a single artist, pianist George Shearing.

With the onslaught brought on by the Beatles' tsunami-like overwhelming of the record industry, Capitol's promotion of its flimsy jazz catalog had been reduced to a trickle. In 1963 the label's best-selling jazz artist was Peggy Lee, whose records were geared more toward pop audiences than to jazz. There was a definite downside to recording for Capitol. Whereas Riverside Records was a boutique label devoted almost exclusively to jazz, Capitol Records' attention was focused on the Beatles and popular vocalists, which almost certainly relegated Adderley to the company's back burner.

Capitol's plan was to exploit the potential of the soul-jazz genre, of which Cannonball Adderley was a progenitor. There was little else going on in jazz at this time—the bossa nova flame was starting to burn out—but Capitol may have seen a glimmer of promise in the success of Adderley singles such as "African Waltz" and was eager to try to "capitol-ize" on Cannonball's popularity in the jazz world. Still, in his eight years with the label, Cannonball struggled, trying to walk a tightrope between the music Capitol wanted him to play and the music he thought his audience would appreciate. The result was a tenuous balance between commercial concerns and Cannonball's own jazz sensibilities.

In an interview in the October 24, 1964, issue of *Billboard*, Cannonball noted that his fans would probably expect him to record with big bands, given that they generally stayed away from small-group jazz recordings. But he expressed a desire to record more with singers—something he was unable to do with Riverside, which concentrated on instrumental performances. Adderley also observed that in his years on the road, he found "too much conformity within the jazz ranks." He also cited his former bandmate John Coltrane, who was able to evolve his own style, despite being "put down by the critics." According to Cannonball, musicians were now overcompensating by actually trying to play noncommercial music. "Musicians are busy analyzing themselves," he said. "They used to enjoy themselves on the stand and this would carry over to their audience. Now jazzmen are injecting 'deliberate complexities' into their styles. It's morally wrong to expect people to pay for satisfying your ego." He encouraged artists not to worry about intellectualizing the way such avant-garde musicians as Ornette Coleman were doing. "Jazz is fun and people should remember this," he concluded.

Capitol assigned the composer and arranger David Axelrod to be in charge of producing Cannonball's recording sessions. Born in 1931, Axelrod was a Los Angeles native who grew up listening to R&B and jazz. In his early years he worked as a chauffeur, boxer, and truck driver, but he was an autodidact when it came to music. After suffering an accident that injured his left hand, he swore he would never do manual labor again. He went to work as a record distributor before landing a job as a producer with a small independent company called Motif Records, a label run as a tax write-off by the oil millionaire Milton W. Vetter. Through the singer Ernie Andrews, Axelrod became friends with jazz keyboardist Gerald Wiggins and produced his first records with Wiggins's trio for Motif.

In 1959, on the recommendation of trombonist Frank Rosolino, Axelrod recorded an album with saxophonist Harold Land for the HiFi label. The album, titled *The Fox*, caused an uproar: it integrated the sound of New York hard bop with the cooler vibe of West Coast jazz. Axelrod was never a fan of West Coast jazz and wanted to record something with a harder edge to it. "Except for Shorty Rogers, I never liked anyone who recorded West Coast jazz, people like Bud Shank or Bill Perkins. I call it 'wet dream music.' You know something happened, but you don't get any gratification from it."

In 1961, while working for Plaza Records on Sunset Boulevard, Axelrod ran into Andrews. The singer introduced him to Cannonball Adderley, who was rehearsing some songs with Andrews for his act. When Cannonball heard Axelrod's name, he extended his hand and said, "*The Fox*! Aha! I knew our paths would cross some day." Axelrod believed that the label's owner, Alan Livingston, was envious of Goddard Leiberson, his counterpart at Columbia, and that that was the main reason he signed Cannonball Adderley.

In 1963 I went to work for Capitol Records and Cannon signed with them about six months after I got there. He was the last really giant name left. Miles was at Columbia, Coltrane had signed with

Impulse, so Alan Livingston went after Cannonball Adderley and got him. Cannon was looking for a major label. If Riverside hadn't gone bankrupt, he would have left anyway. Swifty Lazar made the deal. Swifty was a very powerful figure in the entertainment business. It was a fantastic deal. John Levy never could have gotten the deal for Cannon that Swifty did. Cannon knew Swifty through a man named Ben Shapiro, who owned the Renaissance Club. Cannon used to play there once in a while with Miles. Swifty got him a deal where Cannon was getting a guaranteed $125,000 a year, and that's in 1964. I don't even know what that would be today.

There was nobody like Alan Livingston. Capitol Records would have been the number one grossing label even without the Beatles. Alan took great risks. Sometimes they worked, sometimes they didn't. But I think he loved to take these risks and they were always for a lot of money. The amount of money he gave Cannonball was absurd.

Axelrod had been put in charge of producing the next album by the up-and-coming Chicago soul singer Lou Rawls. Not only had Rawls shown a talent for straddling the line between pop, soul, blues, and jazz, but, like Cannonball Adderley, he was at his best in live settings. He had also developed a hip rapport with his audiences, something that Axelrod no doubt recognized, thanks to his successful live albums for Riverside, as a selling point for Cannonball. *Tobacco Road*, Axelrod's first album with Rawls, became a hit after Axelrod convinced Capitol executives to employ black promotions representatives to plug the album to black radio stations. In the year of the Beatles, Capitol sold half a million copies of *Tobacco Road*.

Cannon's up in Alan Livingston's office talking to Voyle Gilmore, the head of A&R. And Alan told Cannon, "You can have any producer you want, whether it's from here or from outside." And Cannon said, "I'd like David to produce me." It was because of *The Fox*. They thought he meant David Cavanaugh, who did most of the jazz at Capitol. So Alan looked at Voyle and said, "Buzz Cavanaugh and get him up here," and Cannonball held his hand out and said, "No, no, no. David *Axelrod*." And that's how we got started together at Capitol.

Axelrod's first recording featuring the Cannonball Adderley Sextet was taken from a series of concerts at drummer Shelly Manne's Manne-Hole in Los Angeles in the summer of 1964. The album, titled *Cannonball Adderley Live!*, featured four songs, two by Nat Adderley and two by Charles Lloyd, Yusef Lateef's replacement. Axelrod decided to include a recording of the Adderleys' most popular number, "Work Song," along with a new composition by Nat, "Little Boy with the Sad Eyes," on which Lloyd played a screaming avant-garde solo. But *Cannonball Adderley Live!* remained on the drawing board until early 1966, which brought back specters of the disaster at Mercury; two other Adderley LPs were released ahead of it. Axelrod recalled making Cannonball's first album.

> They wanted an album on him rather quick. The guy that actually signed him was a guy named Francis Scott III. Scotty was in business affairs and made up the contracts. He wanted us to record Cannon live. I told him I had to record Kay Starr from eight to eleven and he said "So what? You're young. Go over there and record until two in the morning." So I recorded Kay Starr from eight to eleven that night and then had to beat it over to Shelly's. Luckily, there was a studio on Selma that was owned by Wally Heider, so we just ran cables down the alley from Shelly Manne's into Wally's studio and we set up a camera so I could see Cannon and talk to him and he could talk to me. That was the first album.

In the interim, Capitol released its first attempt at breaking Adderley into the pop singles market when it issued a shortened studio version of "Little Boy with the Sad Eyes" backed with a cover of the theme from the film *Goodbye Charlie*, a popular comedy starring Tony Curtis and Debbie Reynolds. The record went nowhere.

Cannonball's first Capitol single reflected his long-standing struggle with Capitol: one side reflected his own forward-thinking, progressive jazz tendencies, while the other catered to Capitol's targeting of mass-market audiences. A second attempt was made in October when the Quintet (minus Charles Lloyd) recorded a studio session at the Capitol Tower with Ernie Andrews, whose claim to fame was having spent six years singing with the Harry James orchestra.

Four of the ten sides issued on the LP were taken from a Riverside recording made in September 1962 at the Jazz Workshop. After Cannonball signed his contract with Capitol, he provided the label with released and unreleased masters produced by his and Nat's Junat Productions, including five of the eight sides recorded at the Jazz Workshop gig. These were augmented by a live recording made on October 4, 1964, during an afternoon concert at the Lighthouse in Hermosa Beach.

Live Session! Cannonball Adderley with the New Exciting Voice of Ernie Andrews! received a sour report from *Down Beat's* Barbara Gardner, who complained, "It is crass exploitation of an explosive, virile jazz unit to harness it behind a vocalist who has lots of homework to do." Indeed, Andrews's thin voice hardly measured up to the blustering richness of the Adderley Quintet's accompaniment; its sound fell somewhere between that of the blues shouter Joe Turner and the more restrained, cabaret style of Joe Williams, yet retaining neither the excitement of the one nor the intimacy of the other. Axelrod recalled, "It was too haphazard. It was kind of thrown together. We never really discussed it. We just decided to do it. Cannon had great faith in Ernie but finally got sick of him because Ernie had a big mouth and never knew when to keep it shut. Ernie thought he was going to be a big star and take over the group. But it didn't happen."

Two weeks later, with Lloyd back in tow, the Adderley Sextet waded deeper into commercial waters with the unlikely concept of recording songs from 1964's hit Broadway musical *Fiddler on the Roof*. David Axelrod recalled getting a phone call from Cannonball saying that he and Olga had just seen the show and thought it would make a good idea for an album. Axelrod called Tommy Valando (the music's publisher), went to see the show a few days later, and agreed that the music was terrific. Joe Zawinul worked up the arrangements for the Sextet, and the album, which was recorded in New York, came off well—except for one thing. Remembered David Axelrod:

Jerry Bock, who wrote the music for the show, showed up during the session. Bock was terrified that we were going to do some really "out" stuff and destroy his music, so he was very nervous. But after hearing the playback, he loved what he heard. Immediately, he called Reuben's Delicatessen and had them send over all this food; Capitol set up tables in the studios, and they had corned beef, pastrami, brisket, pickles, every kind of bread you could think of, potato salad, cole slaw, it was fantastic. All on Jerry Bock. The funniest thing was that when Jerry got there, he saw Olga, went over and hugged her and they kissed each other on the cheek. Cannon was listening to playbacks, and when he saw this, he looked at me with that Cannonball look and I just shrugged my shoulders. He was so surprised that Jerry knew Olga.

Charles Lloyd was trying to be a cross between Ornette Coleman and John Coltrane. The minute we were done recording the album, Cannon looked at Charles and said, "You're fired. You're through. Get out of here!" Charles was very embarrassed because Cannon fired him in front of me, and I had known Charles for a long time. Cannon had told him not to go into his John Coltrane bag. "Just play," he said. But Charles started playing a thousand notes in every bar when he soloed. Cannon told him, "If that's what I wanted, I'd do it myself."

The premise of the hip Adderley combo playing songs linked to the musical's poverty-stricken 1910 Russian Jewish family seemed preposterous on the surface, but the rhythmic assuredness of the charts helped inspire the musicians to deliver some credibly effective performances, especially on the title track (the show's opener, "Tradition"), on which Cannonball plays an extended solo reminiscent of John Coltrane's iconic performance of another seemingly incompatible property, "My Favorite Things," from Rodgers and Hammerstein's *The Sound of Music*. The celebratory "To Life" actually comes across sounding like a Cole Porter melody (many of Porter's songs were inspired by Jewish themes), swinging with a finger-snapping verve that makes one believe that Adderley could play just about any song and make it his own. In order to capitalize on the still potent influence of the Broadway show, the *Fiddler* album was issued ahead of both the Ernie Andrews collaboration and the live concert at Shelly's Manne-Hole.

In April 1965 Capitol tried painting from a different musical palette by engaging the arranger Oliver Nelson to lead a big-band session featuring Cannonball on alto sax. Nat Adderley and Joe Zawinul were the only other members of the Sextet to be invited to perform on the album, titled *Domination*, which sought to complement the trumpet-and-alto combination with a large orchestra "without intruding upon the virtues of either sound." Olga Adderley recalled that Cannonball blamed the album's lack of success on its clunky programming, especially the placement of "Introduction to a Samba."

David Axelrod tells a fascinating anecdote from the session about the way Cannonball worked with his group:

> The thing I remember from that album was the overtime. We had a twenty-piece band, which was a big band. I remember going over to Cannon and saying, "If we go into overtime, Voyle Gilmore [a senior producer at Capitol Records who was overseeing the session] is going to cut my head off." But Cannon said, "Don't worry about it." Sure enough, we went into overtime. So Clark Terry, who was acting as the contractor, looked at me and said, "Can you get me twenty twenty-dollar bills?" I said, "Yeah, I can do that." So I went back in the booth, called Capitol, and had them sent over to the studio. When the session was over, Clark gave every guy a twenty-dollar bill. Best contractor I ever worked with.

In his brief notes to the album, Cannonball described their approach as an "assault upon the tyranny of style." Once again Nat contributed another superb combination of blues and swing in "Cyclops," in which the orchestra's trumpet and saxophone sections trade two-bar declarations before Cannonball and Nat enter with their own soulful statements, supported by Zawinul's cool pianistic punctuations.

After the first two years of their partnership, Cannonball Adderley and Capitol Records were still without a hit. The mid-1960s was proving to be a precarious time for jazz as the British invasion's hold on public taste intensified. In late 1964 the longtime drummer Louis Hayes left the group to join the Oscar Peterson Trio. Hayes was replaced by Roy McCurdy, who played drums on the Adderley-produced session by the Jazz Brothers (Chuck and Gap Mangione) several years earlier. After working with Betty Carter, Art Farmer, and Sonny Rollins, McCurdy had recently returned to his hometown of Rochester, New York, where he worked as a film tester for Eastman Kodak. He had met Cannonball in the late 1950s while home on leave from a stint with the Air Force.

> I was friends with Chuck Mangione. We all came up together and went to see Cannon's band in Toronto. That's the first time I met him. We hung out in the dressing room with him afterwards. I was discharged in 1959 and went to work in Rochester, New York, with a band that would become Chuck's band, the Jazz Brothers. Cannon had this series called "Cannonball Adderley Presents" on Riverside Records and he would present new artists, so the Jazz Brothers was one of those and we got to know Cannon then. I was playing with Sonny Rollins but I left to come back to Rochester to take care of some personal business, and while I was there, I got a call from Cannon. He said, "Fool, I want you to come join my band." Those were his exact words.
>
> He wanted somebody that could swing and he wanted some fire. He had heard me play before so he knew exactly what he was going to get. But he had to like you, too. And you had to fit in with that Cannonball Adderley Quintet family.

It took McCurdy two weeks to take care of his personal affairs, but Cannonball remained patient, and McCurdy finally joined the band in Atlantic City: "There were no rehearsals. None. We just went straight in and started playing. I got there a couple of days after the gig started. Willie Bobo was playing opposite them so he played drums for a couple of nights until I got there." McCurdy fit in so well with the group that he remained in the band for the rest of Cannonball's life.

Cannonball decided not to replace the volcanic Charles Lloyd, preferring to return to the quintet sound he'd started with back in 1955. Cannonball had already declared his dissatisfaction with the sextet combination, which had peaked during Yusef Lateef's tenure with the group. "I've had it with sextets," he told *Down Beat* in 1964. "The possibilities are only things that somebody else has already done."

In September 1965 Capitol tried assimilating Cannonball's sound with popular music once again when they had the Quintet record a single version of "Like a Rolling Stone," the latest hit by the mercurial folk singer—

turned–rock messiah Bob Dylan. Said David Axelrod, "That wasn't one of my better ideas. . . . It sounded like Morse code." The curious pairing of the Dylan opus with a cover of Earl Wright's soul-flavored instrumental "Thumb a Ride" was even more of a head-scratcher, since Capitol had already issued a single by Wright's orchestra featuring the exact same two songs. It seemed that Capitol had no idea what to do with Adderley and was struggling to find properties that would work for him.

15

THE CLUB

In January 1966 another seminal member of Adderley's Quintet defected: bassist Sam Jones left to join Louis Hayes in Oscar Peterson's organization. The reason was probably financial: Peterson's orchestra was one of the few jazz organizations still doing well in the 1960s, while Adderley's headwind from his Riverside successes appeared to be dying down. Signs of jazz's increasingly lackluster appeal were cropping up all across the country. The Village Gate, formerly a jazz mecca, was now open for business only on weekends. Although the Newport Jazz Festival was still attracting enthusiastic audiences, the nightclub scene for jazz had been replaced, first by folk acts and then by groups spinning off the influence of the Beatles, the Rolling Stones, and pop music's new surge of self-contained garage bands.

Up to this point, however, the Quintet had not been hurting for places to play. Up until the end of 1965 their live concert schedule had seen them engaged in a series of one- to three-week stays at familiar haunts like the Bohemian Caverns in Washington, D.C., the Lighthouse in Los Angeles, and their favorite nightspot, the Jazz Workshop in San Francisco. But after New Year's, dates became more and more widely spaced, with more blank days in their calendar than gigs. In January they played a few days each at the Half Note and the Village Gate before Sam Jones left the group, but that was all. Jones was replaced by Herbie Lewis, a Californian who had played bass on Harold Land's album *The Fox*, a favorite of Cannonball's. After recruiting Lewis to replace Jones, the band experienced two of the driest months in their history.

At this nadir in Cannonball Adderley's career, the flicker of the dying flame was reignited in March 1966 by an engagement the Quintet played at a cavernous new venue in Chicago simply called The Club. It was there that Cannonball realized what had gotten them their success in the first place. It wasn't covering Broadway show tunes, backing big bands, or serving as musical wallpaper for singers, but by playing the funky, blues-soaked music that inspired audiences to clap along and shout encouragement, the "hippy" listeners—the "very important cats"—he had identified in his 1961 column for the *New York Amsterdam News*.

The sound surfaced almost imperceptibly with a pair of singles released by Capitol in the spring of 1966. They had been recorded at a gig at The Club, where Joe Williams had been discovered a generation before, when it was known as Club DeLisa. Located at State Street and Garfield Avenue on Chicago's South Side, it had fallen on hard times since its halcyon days in the 1930s and '40s, when it hosted big bands led by the likes of Fletcher Henderson, Count Basie, and Red Saunders. Along with countless other nightspots, the club fell out of favor with the decline of the big bands and eventually closed in 1958. In early 1966 the building was acquired by two Chicago disc jockeys, E. Rodney Jones and Pervis Spann, and renamed The Club. Jones was working on WVON, one of the top R&B stations in the country, owned by Leonard Chess of Chess Records. To help jump-start his new venue and drum up publicity for it, Jones asked Cannonball Adderley to bring in his Quintet.

By this time Capitol had decided to divide up its A&R duties. Tom Morgan, who had been working for Capitol since the early 1950s and had finally been promoted to the position of vice president of A&R, was assigned as the producer for the sessions held in New York and Chicago. He was told to record Cannonball Adderley's East Coast recordings, but the musician wasn't informed. Toward the end of the gig at The Club, Morgan brought in a Capitol recording unit, but for some reason the recordings he made of the band were put on the shelf, where they remained for nearly forty years. All that was released were two singles, recorded during the last three days of the gig, on March 18, 19, and 20. The singles were scheduled to be part of an album master, but the album was never issued.

Capitol returned to the now-archaic notion of backing Cannonball's

Quintet with an orchestra of strings in arrangements created by Ray Ellis, resulting in the album *Great Love Themes*. Morgan produced this session as well, to Cannonball's chagrin, who always preferred working with David Axelrod. Although Cannonball loved to play show tunes, the lush, watered-down arrangements did not excite listeners, who had long since wearied of the jazz-artist-with-strings formula. Axelrod recalled that Cannonball hated the album and convinced Capitol to let him go back to working with Axelrod from then on.

Full versions of the two edited singles were issued in their entirety thirty-nine years later, when jazz fans were finally permitted a deeper examination of the performances at The Club. It was only then that the reissue producer, Michael Cuscuna, discovered a possible reason that the recordings from the gig had been shelved. One of Cannonball's newer compositions being introduced at The Club was an irresistible uptempo tune called "The Sticks," composed in an unusual fourteen-bar blues pattern. The title, as Cannonball explained to the audience, was not decided upon until the night before the recording was made. "It's a pretty groovy thing," Cannonball joked, "written by one of my favorite people, ladies and gentlemen, Cannonball Adderley." During the gig, small replica drumsticks were distributed to the crowd for the expressed purpose of beating time to the band's funky rhythms. On the recording the audience can be clearly heard pounding noisily on tables, chairs, cocktail glasses, anything within reach. Cannonball gave the audience a lesson in rhythm, instructing them on which beats to hit the sticks from which the song took its title. In the notes to the 2005 reissue on Capitol Jazz, Cuscuna speculated that the incessant drumstick noise was what made Capitol decide not to issue the LP.

The sticks became even more pronounced on Zawinul's "Money in the Pocket," another of the four single sides that had been edited for release and also written as a fourteen-bar blues. What the single version did not contain was a ferocious solo by Nat Adderley on cornet, which ended with the first three phrases from "Work Song." Cannonball's solo took up where Nat's left off, completing Nat's "Work Song" thought and then leading into the first of two solos by Zawinul. The second solo, which came after another restatement of the melody, may have been inspired by Ramsey Lewis's hit recording of "The In Crowd." It consisted of three sections, each beginning quietly, increasing in volume, and then subsiding again, without changing keys. The incessant stick beating followed along, almost engulfing McCurdy's drums. Zawinul worked the crowd masterfully with his funky tour de force yet never lost the groove set down by the rhythm section.

"Money in the Pocket" was backed by a remake of an early composition of Cannonball and Nat's from 1955, "Hear Me Talkin' to You," which was featured on their first album with Kenny Clarke. The edited version of "The Sticks" was backed by the Quintet's closing theme song, Sam Jones's "Unit 7," called "Cannon's Theme" on the single. This was the only song that was not edited for length—the single and album versions were identical. By this time Cannonball was using "Unit 7" for his closing rap to the audience as background music while he introduced the band and then closed the show. (Capitol made the curious decision to issue "Cannon's Theme" on a single, retaining Cannonball's spoken introductions of the Quintet members, something radio disc jockeys were sure not to like.)

Although the unissued concert at The Club had no impact on the Cannonball Adderley Quintet's depleting sales figures in 1966, it served as a clarion call to their roots, the formula that had made them a success in the heady atmosphere of their historic gigs at the Jazz Workshop and the Lighthouse in 1959 and 1960. This musical revival was to bear fruit later in the fall. First, though, they continued to hone their style at a series of personal appearances during the summer, most notably during a return trip to Japan in August, where the biggest hit of Cannonball Adderley's career had its premiere.

16

"WELCOME TO CLUB CAPITOL"

In August 1966 the Cannonball Adderley Quintet began its second tour of Japan. Whereas their first tour in the spring of 1963 saw the band taking a day off in between concerts, there was no time for such extravagances as rest in 1966: the band played twelve dates in a row without a break before returning to Los Angeles for a two-week stay at Shelly Manne's Mann-Hole. The culmination of the tour was a Capitol Records recording of their performance at Sankei Hall in Tokyo on August 26. New to the Quintet was bassist Victor Gaskin, who flew to Japan to replace the departed Herbie Lewis.

Sankei Hall was not unknown to the Quintet. They had recorded the album *Nippon Soul* there during their first Japanese tour, but that was for a different label with a different rhythm section. Only the Adderleys and Joe Zawinul remained from that band. A site of many concerts featuring popular American acts, Sankei Hall was about the size of Carnegie Hall in New York, but the Quintet put on their usual act, as if it were a small club. Like the set at The Club, the song selection included their funkiest, most popular material, a driving "Work Song," the venerable "Bohemia after Dark," and the two songs they had premiered earlier in the year, "The Sticks" and "Money in the Pocket." In the middle of "Jive Samba," Cannonball began quoting Stanley Turrentine's hit "River's Invitation," and Zawinul followed suit, continuing the song's signature riff underneath Nat's cornet solo before returning to the regular melody. The Japanese crowd was polite and attentive, as opposed to the raucous audience at The

Club, but they applauded warmly when Cannonball announced, over quiet riffing from the piano, that they would be playing a new song by Zawinul:

Once again we're happy to be here in Sankei Hall, playing for you, because we have a lot of interesting things to present, like this tune that we're about to play now is a new one written by our pianist, Joe Zawinul. It's a kind of thing based on . . . things in general. There are a lot of things happening now in our country, most of them bad right now. But everything's gonna be all right. The name of this tune is "Mercy . . . Mercy . . . Mercy."

Zawinul wrote the melody for "Mercy, Mercy, Mercy" for a gospel singer whom he was coaching at the time. Its simple theme, played quietly and solemnly, gave way to a more declamatory musical statement that neatly recycled itself back to the initial theme. The song is a modern-day version of the kyrie, a lament impelling black Americans to turn mercy into activism; it is a statement of Zawinul's musical identification with African Americans' struggle for equality. The Japanese crowd applauded appreciatively but most likely did not understand the song's significance (unlike the reception it would get from American audiences when they first heard it several months later). To the Japanese it was simply a bluesy respite that spelled the Quintet's funkier romps that day.

After playing the song again at the Monterey Jazz Festival the next month, the Quintet returned to Los Angeles for a recording session on October 20 at the famed Capitol Tower, on Hollywood's Vine Street, in whose cavernous Studio A David Axelrod had recently recorded a live album with Lou Rawls. Titled *Live!*, the album featured Rawls's hip and humorous spoken introductions to songs such as "Tobacco Road" and "Stormy Monday." It became the biggest hit of Rawls's career, rising to the no. 4 position on *Billboard*'s album charts. (Axelrod wrote one of Rawls's most popular numbers, "Dead End Street," which included an extended rap about growing up in Chicago.) The liner notes implied that the record was made "during an on-stage performance" at a club, but in fact the audience was an elite group of fellow jazz musicians, recording engineers, and people in the business who had been specifically invited to attend. The vibe during the Rawls session helped make the record a huge hit, so Axelrod decided to do the same thing with Cannonball Adderley.

Axelrod and Cannonball, as with Rawls, invited their friends, families, and local jazz musicians to the tower to attend the session. After it was over, Cannonball remembered the ill-fated session at The Club, most of which (except for two singles) would never be issued. He felt that he owed the owners, Jones and Spann, a favor, so he asked Axelrod if he wouldn't mind issuing the album as if it were recorded at The Club. Axelrod agreed and prepared the session:

> I had the band set up on risers and I made it look like a nightclub. I invited the whole Tower. I called the heads of all the departments and said, "We're recording tonight. Get your people to come down." The art department handled the lights, and we had a regular bar set up with two bartenders instead of just having bottles on tables. Well, the place was packed, and when everybody came in, I announced, "Welcome to Club Capitol. Have as much fun as you want. The drinks are free, the food is free, and the music will be great, but remember something. We may do something two times, maybe even three. This is a record date. However, don't let that inhibit you. Show as much life as you want to." So I said, "Okay, Cannon, let's do it." It came across as a live album, which is what it was, but we said something on the back of the album cover that it was recorded in a club in Chicago. We never actually said it so we could be sued, it was kind of intimated that we did. The liner notes were drafted by the legal department. I don't know if that's ever happened before or since. The notes were written by Bob Carp, a brilliant attorney, who wrote them so that it seemed as if the album was recorded in Chicago at The Club. E. Rodney Jones was listed as the notes writer on the album, but E. Rodney was never that hip. I liked him very much but he could never have done that.

The deception was innocent, and it worked. The album, titled *Mercy, Mercy, Mercy! Live at "The Club,"* was deliberately passed off to buyers as something that it was not—a live concert at a raucous club in Chicago instead of the artificial nightclub Axelrod put together in the bowels of the Capitol Tower.

The Studio A parties/recording sessions soon became the hippest tickets in town. Roy McCurdy remembered their genesis: "We recorded the whole night. When the second one came around, they had heard about these things and the crowds got bigger and bigger. It was kind of like an event. Studio A is now cut down into two studios, but it was a huge place at that time."

Mercy, Mercy, Mercy! Live at "The Club" featured six songs. The three on side A were all new numbers: the humorously conjoined titles "Fun" and "Games," both written by Nat Adderley, and Zawinul's "Mercy, Mercy, Mercy." Since the Sankei Hall concert, Zawinul had decided to play "Mercy" on the Wurlitzer electric piano, and the recording at the Capitol Tower was the first time he recorded on the instrument. Cannonball gave the song a typically hip introduction over the shouts of the audience:

> You know, sometimes we're not prepared for adversity. When it happens, sometimes we're caught short. We don't know exactly how to handle it when it comes up. Sometimes we don't know just what to do when adversity takes over. And I have advice for all of us. I got it from my pianist, Joe Zawinul, who wrote this tune. And it sounds like what you're supposed to say when you have that kind of problem. It's called "Mercy . . . Mercy . . . Mercy."

Roy McCurdy remembered that Zawinul experimented first with a Wurlitzer electric piano and finally settled on a Rhodes, with which he could experiment with different effects. Zawinul was always thinking of ways to create different sounds, at one point even shaking his piano to try and get the notes to bend. The band rehearsed the song in Nat Adderley's basement at his home in Teaneck, New Jersey, until they finally got it the way they wanted it. Axelrod recalled, "We used to have these electric pianos lined up against the wall. Joe was always fooling around and playing with them, but he found one that really appealed to him so we used it on the album."

With the audience encouraged to do whatever they felt like doing, the record sounded as though it had been recorded in an old-time southern gospel church. The only solo on "Mercy, Mercy, Mercy" was Zawinul's electric piano, with Cannonball and Nat's horns played only during the statements of the melody. Cannonball had been trying to find a song with a soulful feel that could be a commercial success, and "Mercy, Mercy, Mercy" turned out to be exactly what he was looking for. Roy McCurdy remembered performing it at Jesse Jackson's Operation Breadbasket church in Chicago, where they played regularly; the audiences went crazy for it. David Axelrod recalled hearing the group play the song for the first time at Shelly Manne's Manne-Hole. When the audience got up immediately to dance, he realized that they had something special.

In January 1967 an edited version of "Mercy, Mercy, Mercy" was released on a single (without Cannonball's spoken introduction), backed by the seven-minute long "Games." The single kept climbing the charts until it reached the no. 11 spot, an astounding achievement for a jazz instrumental. The LP, issued a month later, also sold well, reaching no. 13 on the album charts. It was Cannonball's biggest album hit since *Jazz Workshop Revisited* rose to no. 11 in 1963. David Axelrod recalled:

> That record was broken in L.A., not in Chicago. There was a disc jockey on KGFJ at the time called The Magnificent Montague. During the Watts riots in 1965, he was the guy who came up with "Burn, baby, burn." On the air. Unbelievable. One night, I was driving to Capitol to record Letta Mbulu, who was handled by John Levy. I was listening to KGFJ radio and Montague played "Mercy, Mercy, Mercy" seven times in a row. Instead of liking him doing that, I was panicking out of my brain that we were going to get hit for payola! Payola was on everybody's mind then and it usually involved R&B. I said to myself, "Oh my god, what is this guy doing to me?" I got to Capitol and all I could think about was Montague playing Cannon's record seven times in a row. He lay on that album. Capitol gave KGFJ a special plaque when "Mercy, Mercy, Mercy" became a hit. KGFJ broke that album. They were the first ones to play it, not WVON in Chicago.

By this time other soul jazz instrumentals had crept into the pop charts. Some such as Lee Morgan's "The Sidewinder" and Jimmy Smith's "The Cat," even made it to mainstream Top 40 radio stations, but none had the overwhelming success of "Mercy, Mercy, Mercy." Its plaintive, prayerlike melody had the same gospel feel that Ramsey Lewis's "The In Crowd" had going for it in 1965. With rioting in urban centers increasing, the song seemed to be a soothing salve for the turmoil the United States was experiencing in mid-decade. Even before the assassinations of Martin Luther King Jr. and Robert Kennedy turned America into a boiling cauldron two years later, antiwar sentiment against the war in Vietnam and the growing civil disturbances in the nation's major cities were making the United States an angry place to live. "Mercy, Mercy, Mercy" was a plea for civilized reverence at a time when it was in short supply.

David Axelrod remembered that "Mercy, Mercy, Mercy" took off "like a rocket," starting in Los Angeles and then spreading across the country. By the middle of the year the single had sold over 750,000 copies, well on its way to topping a million, while the LP's sales approached 200,000, an unheard-of number for a jazz LP. Cannonball was voted the top alto saxophonist in *Playboy*'s annual jazz poll. Roy McCurdy remembered driving cross-country from New York to Los Angeles with the band and hearing "Mercy" played on the all-night jazz radio programs for months.

Four sets of lyrics were eventually published to go with Zawinul's melody. The first, by Gail Fisher, John Levy's wife, and John's oldest son, Vincent, were written with Nancy Wilson in mind. The chorus went:

> *Baby have some mercy*
> *Please don't make me beg on bended knees*
> *Oh please, mercy, mercy, mercy,*
> *Please have mercy on me.*
> *Mercy, mercy, mercy please.*

A second set was written by Eddie Jefferson, a singer known for writing words to go with improvised jazz solos. The third set, which became the most famous, was written by the R&B/soul singer Larry Williams and Johnny "Guitar" Watson, who recorded their version on a Columbia LP titled *Two for the Price of One*. This set of lyrics was picked up by an American pop/rock quintet called the Buckinghams, who rode to the Top 10 with their version. After Cannonball's death, a fourth version was written by David Olivia for Zawinul's group, the Zawinul Syndicate. Retitled "No

Mercy for Me (Mercy, Mercy, Mercy)," it appeared on the group's 1988 album *The Immigrants*.

Capitol Records was shocked but delighted with the success of "Mercy, Mercy, Mercy," and in March 1967 the Quintet was hustled back into the studio to record a follow-up, which they hoped would satisfy the demands for more songs in that vein. Once again the audience was a contrived one. Axelrod, possibly feeling guilty about the deception behind the *Mercy, Mercy, Mercy* LP, this time put quotations around the word "live" on the back of the album jacket ("Another great 'live' album in their *Mercy, Mercy, Mercy* groove!") without revealing the nature of the audience or the venue where the concert was recorded. The Quintet once again used the soul-jazz formula, leading off with a rambunctious recording of Curtis Fuller's "Mini Mama," with Zawinul stimulating the audience's rhythmic handclapping with his electric piano groove.

The other two songs recorded that day would be issued on a single. The A side was "Why (Am I Treated So Bad?)," written by Roebuck "Pops" Staples, patriarch of the Chicago gospel group the Staple Singers. The song had the same churchy feel as "Mercy, Mercy, Mercy" and was similarly constructed—a slow drag with a soulful melody in the same fourteen-bar blues structure as "Money in the Pocket" and "The Sticks." After Cannonball and Nat played the melody, Zawinul took four successive choruses on electric piano, accompanied by ecstatic shrieks, yells, and shouts from the invited audience. The single version was edited down from nearly eight minutes to a more radio-friendly three.

The B side of the single was "I'm On My Way," written and arranged by Nat Adderley's eleven-year-old son Nat Jr., a budding pianist and composer in his own right. This time Zawinul returned to playing standard piano, allowing Cannonball and Nat to stretch their solos out. The record is one of the tours de force of the Quintet's career, an exciting, driving number in which the three solos built on one another to create a masterpiece of infectious fury. It began with a highly melodic chorus by Cannonball on alto sax, which gave way to a fiery Spanish-tinged sequence by Nat on cornet. Zawinul's bluesy chorus on piano kept the momentum up, and by the time it was over he had the crowd clapping along and screaming in orgiastic delight. After the song was finished the crowd erupted in enthusiastic applause and yells, and all the usually articulate Cannonball could say was, "I declare. I do declare." Axelrod decided it would have been anathema to edit "I'm On My Way" to the normal two-and-a-half to three-minute duration of the average 45-rpm single. Taking any of the solos out would have destroyed the build-up, so he crammed all seven minutes and five seconds of it onto the B side of the 45 single, without editing a note out.

The LP *Why Am I Treated So Bad!* is also notable in that it featured a new closing theme song for the group: "The Scene," co-written by Nat Adderley and Joe Zawinul. But despite another solid lineup of songs in Cannonball's soul-jazz vein, the album failed to achieve the same crossover status as *Mercy, Mercy, Mercy*, not even cracking the Top 100.

The Quintet had one more recording session in 1967, with another attempt made to cash in on the "Mercy, Mercy, Mercy" sound. The song, titled "Walk Tall," was co-written by Zawinul with gospel singer "Queen" Esther Marrow and James Rein, and again featured Zawinul's electric piano in a slow, soulful melody. Cannonball introduced the number using his familiar hip preach-talk: "Like I said before, there are times when things don't lay the way they're supposed to lay. But regardless, you're supposed to hold your head up high and walk tall. Walk TALL!" Unlike its predecessors, "Mercy, Mercy, Mercy" and "Why (Am I Treated So Bad)," "Walk Tall" had no improvisations by the Quintet. This song did not resonate with audiences, although it was added to the group's regular concert repertoire.

"Walk Tall" was included on the LP *74 Miles Away*, whose title song was penned by the group's "musical chameleon," as Cannonball described Zawinul to a Paris audience in 1969: "He turns up in different musical colors daily. I never know what he's gonna be thinking about. Maybe that's a good idea. That way he shouldn't get hung up like the rest of us." "74 Miles Away" was a fourteen-minute epic that got its name from its quirky 7/4 time signature, which showed the new direction the Quintet was heading during the Summer of Love, in which psychedelia and the increasingly sophisticated rock scene were beginning to have an influence on jazz.

The combination of rock elements with jazz was to become known as fusion, a style pioneered by Joe Zawinul and Miles Davis. Reaching its full, mature expression with the release of Davis's landmark album *Bitches Brew* in 1970, fusion would soon replace soul jazz and hard bop as the direction of jazz in the 1970s, and Cannonball Adderley would soon follow that path as well, experimenting with more diverse music than ever before.

"74 Miles Away" (the word "miles" may have been an oblique if not appropriately accidental reference to Davis) had a strange, Middle Eastern–flavored melody featuring Nat alternately growling and shrieking into his cornet and Zawinul achieving an exotic Turkish effect by placing a tambourine on the strings of his piano during his solo. Roy McCurdy recalled:

> He was still thinking about trying to get a different sound; the sounds you couldn't get because the electric things weren't really in there at that time. They came in a little later, where you could do a lot of different things and put a lot of different sounds and colors in there. Joe was very intense and an incredible player. He was probably a genius. But he played his butt off, all the time.

In 1968 Cannonball turned forty, an age he never thought he would live to see. That year saw the beginning of some startling changes in Cannonball's music as he made his first explorations into the avant-garde and jazz's African roots. Soul jazz would remain part of his repertoire for the remainder of his career, but these were his "borrowed time" years, and Cannonball Adderley was going to make the best of them by making musical and sociological statements not only in his work, but also outside his musical life.

17

ACCENT ON AFRICA

The late 1960s was one of the worst periods for jazz in its history. Nightclubs and other venues for jazz had been dying out for years, and except for the occasional commercial hit, most youngsters grew up without being exposed to it. This concerned Cannonball Adderley, which was one reason why he continued his practice of visiting schools, delivering lectures on jazz, conducting clinics, and serving as a judge at jazz festivals. The Adderley Quintet was one of the few jazz groups that flourished in the latter part of the decade, thanks in chief to the phenomenal success of "Mercy, Mercy, Mercy." Although his brother Nat enjoyed the limelight and had no problem playing and replaying "Mercy," "Work Song," and the other Adderley signature songs, Cannonball had grandiose plans for expanding his base, experimenting with avant-garde sounds and styles, and trying to push the envelope.

In 1968 Cannonball made several significant changes to his life and his music. In the spring he and Olga moved from their home on Long Island to Los Angeles, where they would be closer to Capitol Records' headquarters. On his next album he decided to play soprano saxophone, an instrument he had only dabbled with previously, rarely if ever playing it in concert. In addition, he started experimenting with the Varitone, a device that could be attached to the neck of an instrument that could not only amplify its sound, but also provide interesting and novel effects, including tremolo, echo, and even division of the sound into parallel octaves. The Varitone had been introduced by the renowned musical instrument company Selmer in 1965 and became a regular part of the repertoire of saxophonists Eddie Harris, Lou Donaldson, and Sonny Stitt. Cannonball was intrigued with the sound, which he thought would go perfectly with an album of music from Africa that he was preparing.

The highlife sound of West Africa, characterized by the use of jazz horns, had been infused by the popularity of soul music in the 1960s. Jazz musicians from Africa found Great Britain a receptive country for their music, and it was only a matter of time before the United States, which with the Beatles' invasion had begun looking to Britain for musical direction, would be introduced to African music as well. The performance by South African trumpeter Hugh Masekela at the 1967 Monterey Pop Festival helped spur the popularity of African jazz in the United States, which came to a head when Masekela's instrumental "Grazing in the Grass" topped both the pop and R&B charts in the summer of 1968.

In June, with Masekela's single zooming up the charts, Cannonball joined forces with an orchestra led by conductor and arranger H. B. Barnum for an album that would be called *Accent on Africa*. As Cannonball explained in the liner notes, the album was "meant to show the influence rather than the pure form of African sources." As a result, most of the exotic-sounding song titles (taken from words in the Zulu, Sesotho, and Swahili languages) were actually written by the usual suspects: Cannonball, Nat, and Zawinul, with one ("Up and At It") composed by guitarist Wes Montgomery. (The day after the session concluded, Montgomery died of a heart attack at the young age of forty-five.)

Two of the album's songs ("Khutsana" and "Gumba Gumba") were penned by the South African songwriter Caiphus Semenya, whose wife, Letta Mbulu, would become a protégé of Cannonball's in the 1970s. The Johannesburg-born Mbulu had made her triumphant American debut at the Village Vanguard in 1964 before moving to Los Angeles, where she joined fellow African performers Hugh Masekela and Miriam Makeba in a concert at Hollywood's Huntington Hartford Theatre. In 1967, after playing at the Ash Grove in Los Angeles and the hungry i in San Francisco, Mbulu was signed to a contract by Capitol Records.

The songs on *Accent on Africa* had a multilayered sound highlighted by infectious melodies, an aspect that was particularly attractive to the commercially minded Cannonball. Semenya's jubilant "Gumba Gumba" and Cannonball's medium-tempo swinger "Hamba Nami" were selected for the two sides of the single release; not coincidentally, these two numbers also featured Cannonball's use of the Varitone. Cannonball's first use of the soprano sax came on a tune Axelrod wrote called "Gun-Jah." *Down Beat* called *Accent on Africa* a "damn good LP," full of swinging arrangements and high spirits, and compared Cannonball's Varitone to an "alley viola." The critic Ira Gitler, however, never an Adderley fan, complained that "Adderley's group has really become showbiz. Their African tunes made them look like a commercial gospel group." Cannonball took the African imagery beyond the musical element, discarding the formal suit and tie he had always worn and donning colorful West African dashikis in performance and on the album's cover. As he got older, his musical explorations became more pronounced, almost restless, as he moved from one genre to another, always seeking out new ways to communicate the music he was in a constant state of learning himself.

On August 6 the Quintet began a three-week gig at the London House in Chicago. The end of the engagement coincided with the start of the Democratic National Convention, which was being held at the International Amphitheatre on the city's South Side. The London House was located near the corner of State Street and Wacker Drive, about seven miles north of the Amphitheatre. Roy McCurdy recalls seeing helmeted policeman preventing crowds from crossing the Chicago River at State Street to get to the club. (The infamous riots took place on Wednesday, August 28, three days after the band finished their stretch at the London House.)

Racial strife was still a big problem for touring bands in the late 1960s. McCurdy remembered that for the first several years he played with the band, segregation was still enforced in southern cities like Atlanta and Memphis. When they played in the South, the band was forced to stay in "black hotels," and band members were not permitted to swim in pools where whites swam. Joe Zawinul, the only white member of the band, supported his bandmates by staying wherever they stayed. By 1970 the protests and riots began to have a positive effect, and the restrictions placed on blacks began to loosen up. Cannonball would talk about racial issues often, even onstage, but he always couched his remarks with his own wry sense of humor and intelligent outlook.

On September 23, 1968, the Quintet returned to the Capitol Tower for another live session before an invited audience. Recalled Roy McCurdy, "By the time we did our third album there, there were hundreds waiting, I mean there was just a crowd outside Capitol Records trying to get in for this thing. So we were recording and Nancy [Wilson] and Lou Rawls were in the audience. So Cannon called them both up to just spontaneously do some things." After introducing Rawls, Cannonball wryly commented, "You come to our record sessions, there ain't no telling who's gonna show up. We're expecting Tennessee Ernie any minute. Or Buck Owens." Rawls announced the birth of his daughter and joined the band for the swinging blues number "I'd Rather Drink Muddy Water." Wilson, whom Cannonball had discovered in 1959, sang Buddy Johnson's ballad "Save Your Love for Me."

The Quintet completed the album, which was titled *In Person* (again in quotes) at a second session on October 7, in which two new compositions that had been introduced at the first session were rerecorded, Joe Zawinul's driving "Rumpelstiltskin" (which featured an exuberant divided-octave solo by Cannonball with the Varitone) and Nat's "Sweet Emma," a slow gospel-flavored number that paid tribute to the seventy-one-year-old New Orleans jazz pianist Emma Barrett, who had recently suffered a debilitating stroke.

Despite their popularity as a touring group, the Cannonball Adderley Quintet would not record for another year. In the spring of 1969 they embarked on an extensive tour of Europe that had them playing dates in France, Austria, Sweden, Norway, Germany, Italy, and Belgium. On March 27, at the Musicorama festival at the Salle Pleyel in Paris, the band had just completed a performance of "Manha de Carnaval," the exquisite and evocatively beautiful theme from *Black Orpheus*, when they were unexpectedly greeted not with cheers and applause, but with a chorus of boos from the audience. The booing became so threatening that Cannonball gestured for the band to leave the stage until it subsided. Roy McCurdy recalled that Cannonball was both angry and confused by the unexpected reaction. They later found out that "Manha de Carnaval" had been adopted by one of the Arab factions that was against Charles de Gaulle's efforts to rebuild relations between France and the Arab states. The performance was recorded and released in 1992 on the French RTE label, with the offending song mistitled "Black Orpheus."

Upon returning the Quintet played a highly charged date at the Club Baron in Harlem, with Letta Mbulu joining them. After this gig Victor Gaskin left the group; he remained in New York to play with Duke Ellington and then Thelonious Monk. Replacing him was Walter Booker, who had played with Sonny Rollins in the early 1960s. Olga Adderley believed that it was Booker's arrival that signaled the group's change in concert attire.

That summer Joe Zawinul participated in a Miles Davis recording session that would result in the landmark album *Bitches Brew*. At the session, Zawinul met saxophonist Wayne Shorter. Finding that they shared many ideas about the new fusion movement, the two began talking about a cooperative venture that would later see the Austrian pianist depart the Cannonball Adderley Quintet after more than nine years of service.

18

COUNTRY PREACHER

In the fall of 1968 the Cannonball Adderley Quintet was invited to be artists-in-residence during Black Heritage Week at Georgia's Albany State College, an all-black school. In the group's frequent visits to high schools and colleges, Cannonball had become disturbed by how little black Americans knew about their own musical roots. "It's amazing to find so many black people who are not interested in jazz at all," he told the *New York Times*. "When college kids book a group, they don't care whether it's jazz, only whether it's popular. What matters, is, are you on the charts?"

Cannonball used the group's popularity to help educate young African Americans by offering a two-day program of lectures, seminars, and demonstrations on black music free to every college where the group was booked for a concert. On the first day Cannonball would lead a discussion with the students on the chronological evolution of black music. When the inevitable question "What is black music?" was asked, Cannonball's simple answer was, "Music created by and oriented to black people."

The second day would feature discussions of the sociocultural significance of black music and its effect on current popular musical trends. Qualified music students were able to participate in individual clinics conducted by the members of the Quintet. In 1969 the program was presented at a variety of schools, including Savannah State College in Georgia, Florida A&M University (Cannonball's alma mater), Lanay College in Oakland, California, and West Virginia University.

The members of the Cannonball Adderley Quintet all joined their leader in assisting with the programs. Each was given a different topic to research and would then be asked to conduct individual seminars at the schools. Roy McCurdy, who studied percussion at the Eastman School of Music in Rochester, New York, gave lectures on African instruments and rhythm. Joe Zawinul, a graduate of the Vienna Conservatory, discussed the differences between European and African musical styles, explained the different kinds of scales used in each, and demonstrated the differences between Arab scales and the qualities of blue notes. As the only white person in the band, Zawinul came prepared for any probing and potentially embarrassing question, such as "Can a white person have soul?," to which Zawinul would respond indignantly, "Are you kidding?"

Nat Adderley, who studied brass instruments at Florida A&M, covered the sociological aspects of black music, while Cannonball coordinated the entire series, handing out a bibliography of resources to study, a recommended list of recordings, and other instructional materials. In his inimitably breezy fashion, Cannonball crowed, "By the first of the year, we'll have a syllabus in print and then we ought to be really swinging." This remarkable educational series continued until the end of Cannonball's life.

In March 1969 Cannonball became a cofounder of the Black Academy of Arts and Letters, an assemblage of fifty scholars, artists, and performers organized to accord recognition to those making "notable" contributions to black culture. Among the others named to the committee were the actors Ossie Davis and Sidney Poitier, the historian John Hope Franklin, the dancer and choreographer Alvin Ailey, and the painter Floyd Coleman. In his founding address C. Eric Lincoln, an author and professor of religion and sociology at the Union Theological Seminary in New York, said, "Soul is the essence of blackness. It is the creative genius of the liberated men and women who have come to terms with themselves and with their black heritage. If black is beautiful, it is soul that makes it so. If what is black can also be excellent, the Black Academy of Arts and Letters is long overdue."

By the end of 1969 Cannonball Adderley had become not just a popular nightclub and festival act, but a leader in his field, who helped spread the pride of his heritage as an African American with other Americans of all races. He had been associated with Operation Breadbasket, the economic arm of the Southern Christian Leadership Conference, since shortly after its founding in 1962, playing concerts for events and occasionally giving speeches about music education. Operation Breadbasket dedicated itself to improving the economic conditions of black communities in the United States. Martin Luther King Jr. had served as the organization's president until he was murdered in 1968. In 1966 the SCLC selected the Reverend Jesse Jackson to head the Chicago chapter of Operation Breadbasket. He would remain with the organization until December 1971, when he had a falling-out with Ralph Abernathy, King's successor at the SCLC; Jackson then formed Operation PUSH (People United to Save Humanity), now known as the Rainbow Coalition.

Jackson extended an open invitation for Cannonball to play for Operation Breadbasket on any Sunday the band was in Chicago. On October 17 and 18, 1969, the Cannonball Adderley Quintet recorded an album for Capitol Records at a church on Chicago's South Side. Jackson himself was present, supplanting Cannonball's usual role as raconteur by introducing some of the performances. Joe Zawinul wrote a tune dedicated to Jackson called "Country Preacher," which began with a soulful melody played by Cannonball on alto, backed by Zawinul's understated electric piano, that burst into a declamatory hallelujah fanfare before returning to the low, reverent melody. The sudden transitions from soft to loud made the crowd explode with a roar of approval at several points during the song.

Roy McCurdy remembered sitting at the drums behind Cannonball and Nat, who always fronted the band, and performing "Country Preacher" live: "They were really funny to me because I was behind them all the time, looking at them. Nat was short and Cannon was tall. And they both had a way of snapping their fingers and moving, and their behinds were both in sync. During that pause, that's what was going on. And then they'd go back and hit it. Joe would hit it and the people loved that thing. It was kind of a follow-up to 'Mercy, Mercy, Mercy.'"

"Country Preacher" was issued on a single, backed by "Hummin'," a Nat Adderley tune with a marchlike rhythm that escalated into a thrilling gospel groove. Nat explained that the song's rhythm was inspired by the memory of an old woman named Miss Sally who lived on the Adderleys' street in Tallahassee when they were growing up. Miss Sally made a habit of sitting in a rocking chair on her front porch, rocking while shelling peas.

There was a loose floorboard in the porch, and as she was rocking, she would hum "little churchy sounding things," punctuated by the rhythm of the loose board banging back and forth. Sometime later, Nat said that he was taken to task by his mother, who asked him why he never wrote any songs with meaning, like "Stardust." He told her about Miss Sally inspiring "Hummin'," but she didn't buy it. Then one night Nat invited her to come see the Quintet perform at the Village Gate. After the band played "Hummin'," Mrs. Adderley called Nat over to her table and admitted that he was right—the rhythm did remind her of old Miss Sally. "Now that I see that, I'm gonna get off your case," she told her son. Said Nat, "That's when I knew Momma was hip."

David Axelrod's departure from Capitol in April 1970 had a heavy impact on Cannonball Adderley, although the two remained close friends until Adderley's death. Axelrod left Capitol two years after Alan Livingston left to form his own company, Mediarts. Livingston's exit resulted in a series of defections from the company, including that of Lou Rawls, one of the label's biggest stars, who signed to record for M-G-M. Axelrod recalled that Livingston's departure followed an argument with Sir Joseph Lockwood, the president of EMI in London. According to Axelrod, Capitol was never the same after Livingston left.

> It caught us all by surprise. We all went into shock. No Alan. A couple of years before Lou Rawls died, I asked him if he would have stayed at Capitol if Alan Livingston had stayed and he said, "You're damn right I would have. I left because Livingston was no longer there." I said, "That's weird, so did I." They didn't want me to leave either. It wasn't the same place. It shows you the effect one person can have on a big corporation.

Although Axelrod had left Capitol, he signed a production deal with the label enabling him to continue producing Cannonball Adderley's albums.

While performing a three-week engagement at the Hong Kong Bar at the Century Plaza Hotel in Los Angeles, Cannonball Adderley participated in what was possibly his most ambitious project to date: a session combining the Quintet with the Los Angeles Philharmonic, led by the arranger and conductor William Fischer. Fischer was a pioneer of jazz fusion, most notably combining jazz with classical music on Herbie Mann's "Concerto Grosso in D Blues," which was released on Atlantic Records in 1968. Now Fischer was ready to do something similar with Cannonball Adderley. The result was "Experience in E," a twenty-minute-long musical conundrum in which Cannonball journeyed to the outer limits of the avant-garde, showing that he had the capacity for emulating John Coltrane as much as he did the soul jazz of Horace Silver. (Fischer later claimed that Zawinul wrote only the introduction and that Fischer himself was responsible for the bulk of the piece.) The work includes Nat Adderley's now frequent experimentations with the alien sounds he could produce from his cornet, idiosyncratic bass playing by Walter Booker, and a variety of other fascinating effects, including an extraordinary section featuring the orchestra's string section playing pizzicato.

The other side of the record featured "Dialogues for Jazz Quintet and Orchestra," a twelve-and-a-half-minute piece written by the jazz composer and arranger Lalo Schifrin that further pushed the definitions of jazz, anticipating even more experimentation to come in the 1970s. Rounding out the album was another avant-garde work, "Tensity," which had been composed by David Axelrod in anticipation of its being performed at that year's Monterey Jazz Festival. Axelrod's seventeen-year-old son Scott had just died, and Cannonball told him that he needed to compose the work to help him cope with his grief. Axelrod recalled: "If you want to hear what I think is one of the best saxophone solos ever—forget about alto or tenor, whatever—Cannon took a solo on "Tensity" that is so insane and so great, my mouth was open in the booth. Nobody could believe it, it was so incredible."

A more conventional album followed, *The Price You Got to Pay to Be Free*, released as a double-disc gatefold album, which became a favorite format for Cannonball in the last years of his life. The record, which included performances from a live appearance at the Monterey Jazz Festival on September 19, 1970, ran the gamut of Cannonball's musical spectrum. There was Brazilian, soul jazz, avant-garde, and even some political posturing by a guest vocalist—Nat Adderley Jr., now fifteen, who made his professional debut singing the title track. Cannonball introduced the number, saying, "Let me let you know how a young black American— fifteen years old—feels about life in the United States for himself, today."

The song was surprisingly pointed and angry for one so young, with an appropriately placed epithet showing that the wounds inflicted on black Americans by the assassination of Martin Luther King Jr. were still festering.

Capitol's Studio A was undergoing renovations, so the studio recordings on the album were made at A&M Records' large recording studio. *The Price You Got to Pay to Be Free* is also noteworthy for featuring the only vocal performances by the Adderley brothers: on Milton Nascimento's "Bridges," which was highlighted by a psychedelic intro played on a synthesizer. Cannonball's vocal was surprisingly effective and tender in a piece uncharacteristic of what his audiences were used to hearing. It is unfortunate that this effective number proved to be the only example we have of Cannonball's singing ability.

Also on the album was a recording of Axelrod's "Tensity," recorded on September 20 at Monterey in a performance led by Axelrod himself, after strenuous efforts on the part of both Cannonball and Booker to convince the petrified neophyte conductor to do so. He received a standing ovation after the performance, although the *Down Beat* critic Harvey Siders said that Axelrod "revealed his inability to handle large forces." Axelrod left Capitol shortly after completing the recording of *The Price You Got to Pay to Be Free* in the first week in October.

The final sessions for the album would prove to be the last appearance made by Joe Zawinul on a Cannonball Adderley album. Two months later, on December 15, Zawinul announced that he was leaving the Quintet to start a new band with Wayne Shorter, to be called Weather Report. Zawinul's departure had apparently been imminent for some time. The seeds of it were most likely planted during Miles Davis' *Bitches Brew* sessions in 1968, when Zawinul first met Shorter and began talking about their common aspirations. The Adderleys, who grew up in a close-knit family, were understandably upset at Zawinul's calculated escape. The trusting Nat was especially injured by the defection, claiming in a 1990 interview that it seemed "to have been plotted in an underhand manner." Roy McCurdy recalled, "He got a chance to really show his thing when he started Weather Report, but he had been talking about that kind of music two or three years before he left the band, things he wanted to do and the direction he wanted to go in."

During his nine and a half years with the Quintet, Joe Zawinul had left an indelible imprint on the group's sound. For one thing, he had written most of the band's commercial successes, most notably their signature hit, "Mercy, Mercy, Mercy." He would go on to make even greater strides on his own, helping to instigate the fusion between jazz and rock in the 1970s and becoming a hugely influential figure in jazz. David Axelrod remembered that Zawinul's exit was not an easy one for the group:

> Joe didn't give Cannon any notice. I liked Joe a lot, but that was really wrong. He had been planning on leaving for some time with Wayne Shorter and Miraslov Vitous. The three of them had planned it for quite a while. But Cannon ended up getting George Duke, and George brought a different feeling to the group. George could never play as good as Joe, but he didn't have to, because he had different things to say. He was very much R&B influenced and Cannon really liked that a lot.

As for the Adderleys, they could only press on. In February 1971 the Quintet became a sextet once again when Cannonball added avant-garde guitarist Sonny Sharrock, who had been working for Herbie Mann. Sharrock did not remain long, however, although Cannonball would use electric guitarists more frequently in future efforts, following the jazz fusion roadmap.

Zawinul's departure did not sway Cannonball Adderley from his plans to experiment with different kinds of grander works. He no longer felt obliged to cater to Capitol Records' demands to achieve commercial success with hit singles. That would soon lead to his departure from the label. One of his final efforts for Capitol would come next, in which he would combine all of the musical elements of his previous recordings into one singularly ambitious project.

19

THE BLACK MESSIAH

As the 1970s began, the jazz-rock evolution that was developing was having a pronounced effect on the Cannonball Adderley Quintet. First, its dulcet siren song called Joe Zawinul to uncharted waters as he sailed off with his new band. But Cannonball was not far behind, and in 1971 he attacked the new trend head-on with his own take on the electronic jazz-rock explosion, which he felt was a key to attracting a new, younger, and more vibrant audience.

Although Zawinul had been testing the waters for some time now with new ways of playing jazz on electronic keyboards, George Duke had plunged in with both feet, and on the Adderleys' next album Duke was given free rein to utilize new electronic gadgets like the ring modulator and the Echoplex.

Ring modulation was first employed in 1956 by the German avant-garde composer Karlheinz Stockhausen. Since then it had been used in a variety of circumstances to process combinations of sounds for keyboards, guitars, and even voices. Its purpose was to combine more than one audio signal with the output, creating two waveforms in what Stockhausen described as "colored noise." Ring modulators had been used increasingly in the rock world by such groups as Black Sabbath and the Grateful Dead. It was one of the earliest devices that, instead of capturing sounds, created new, synthetic ones.

The Echoplex is a device used to create a tape-delay effect. It was built in 1959 by Mike Battle, who originally intended it for use by guitar players.

First marketed in the early 1960s, the Echoplex was used by musicians such as Chet Atkins, Les Paul, and Jimmy Page, but keyboard players soon began using it as well.

Cannonball had recently conducted a thirty-eight-piece orchestra in David Axelrod's rock adaptation of George Frederic Handel's *Messiah*, which incorporated elements of gospel, blues, jazz, and rock. The album would be released on the RCA label later that year. The next album by the Quintet was another double album, recorded live at the Troubadour nightclub in West Hollywood. Well-known as a haven for folk and rock music, the Troubadour was nonetheless an unlikely place to record a live album of jazz, much less one with the experimental sounds Cannonball Adderley was preparing, but Cannonball made sure to augment his Quintet with rock musicians who would help bridge the musical gap: clarinetist Alvin Batiste, reedman Ernie Watts, rock guitarist Mike Deasy, Brazilian percussionist Airto Moreira, and African drummer Buck Clarke. (Cannonball announced to the assemblage, "Now I don't give a damn whether you can count or not, we still are the Cannonball Adderley Quintet!")

The album, titled *The Black Messiah*, was recorded during a week's worth of shows at the Troubadour between August 3 and 9, 1971. The album incorporated Cannonball's most eclectic and diverse combination of styles yet, with elements of rock, soul, jazz, blues, funk, and avant-garde in a constantly changing onrush of musical sounds. Deasy and Clarke were featured on many tracks, including the raucous "Little Benny Hen," the avant-garde "Zenek," and the otherworldly-sounding "The Steam Drill," whose title, a reference to the folk legend of John Henry, presaged *Big Man*, the last work Cannonball completed before his death. Cannonball indulged his new fascination with the soprano sax on the album as well as Nat's own exploration of the different guttural noises he could get out of his cornet.

The album did not lack the influence of the departed Zawinul: it included the pianist's "Dr. Honoris Causa" (Latin for "honorary degree"), a fourteen-minute atmospheric tribute to the keyboardist Herbie Hancock, which Zawinul himself would record on his self-titled album for Atlantic, also released in 1971. There was also Cannonball's tribute to fellow alto saxophonist Paul Desmond in the tune "Pretty Paul." Eight tracks recorded at the Troubadour session were held back for what would be Cannonball's final Capitol release, *Music, You All*, which wasn't released until 1976, a year after his death. Unlike *Bitches Brew*, *The Black Messiah* did not find an audience, in part because Capitol listed it at full price, rather than discounting it as they did for other multiple-album sets. It remains an intriguing and overlooked remnant from the early days of jazz-rock fusion.

In live performance, Cannonball Adderley made sure not to totally alienate his loyal fan base by spacing his more abstract, electronics-filled experiments apart from his litany of soul-jazz hits. He kept pace with Miles Davis by continuing to present these ideas in concert, touring with John McLaughlin's similarly forward-thinking Mahavishnu Orchestra in 1971 and 1972.

In January 1972 another "Cannonball Adderley Presents" album was recorded at the Capitol Tower, this one under his brother Nat's name. *Soul Zodiac* contained a series of twelve musical vignettes topped off by astrological musings by the Los Angeles disc jockey Rick Holmes. Beneath the superfluous narration lay a wide variety of eclectic musical styles, ranging from jazz and rock to outer-spacey electronics rife with echo and tape loops. Ernie Watts took Cannonball's role on sax; Cannonball made token appearances on only two tracks, "Aries" and "Libra."

On July 31, 1972, Cannonball made his last album for Capitol Records to be issued under his own name, nostalgically recording it at Studio A in the Capitol Tower, the locale for his most successful records for the label. As before, a handpicked audience was present, providing the party atmosphere that generated excitement and enthusiasm from the band. The album, titled *The Happy People*, was a musical left turn for Cannonball, who had been moving inexorably toward the avant-garde sounds evidenced on *The Black Messiah*. Instead, *The Happy People* surprised his fans by focusing on the exuberant music of Brazil during Carnival time, the Quintet augmented by the inclusion of percussionists King Errisson, Airto Moreira, and Mayuto Octavio, as well as with vocalist Flora Purim. Cannonball's wife, Olga, an actress who usually steered clear of her husband's musical life, contributed an idiosyncratic vocal on "Savior," for which she wrote the lyrics to Cannonball's melodic line. Roy McCurdy recalled:

We had just come back from Brazil; we had gone down there for the first time and just had an amazing time, meeting all their people and playing with all these great musicians. We met Milton

Nascimento and Jobim and we hung out in Jobim's apartment all the time and all these wild parties were going on. So when we came back, Cannon wanted to do this Brazilian album. We were really close with Airto so we did this album called *The Happy People.*

Moreira's title track and Milton Nascimento's "Maria Três Filhos" were both extended, high-octane rhythmic jams, with unison group vocals and Cannonball's sax dancing over the Carnival atmosphere.

Like Carnival, the studio had a raucous and exuberant atmosphere, bringing back memories of the small nightclubs in New York Cannonball played when he was just starting out. David Axelrod returned as coproducer, while Nat Adderley Jr. provided an arrangement for the Brazilian composer Benito Di Paula's celebratory "Ela," featuring a vocal by Airto Moreira. *The Happy People* added the extra dimension of world music to the musical cocktail that Cannonball had been experimenting with for the past several albums.

Down Beat praised the album for its "happy, noisy, and rhythmic" atmosphere, but by that time, the bloom was off the rose for Cannonball and Capitol Records. With no further hits forthcoming and Cannonball's music departing more and more from the soul-jazz successes of the mid-1960s, his contract was not renewed at the end of 1972. One final session remained, which was released under Nat Adderley's name. The album, titled *Cannonball Adderley Presents: Soul of the Bible,* was another departure from the norm, a concept album presenting a soul-angled exploration of themes from the Bible, again narrated by the Los Angeles disc jockey Rick Holmes. (Cannonball would use Holmes's talents for a third time on his 1974 album *Love, Sex & the Zodiac.*)

Recorded on October 14, 1972, *Soul of the Bible* was an uneven mix of styles, with funky rhythms provided by the percussionists from the *Happy People* LP, meandering instrumental solos, and a return to jazz fusion. Each song was prefaced by Holmes's seductive readings from scripture. "Fun in the Church," which featured a pulsating rhythm and a vocal by Fleming Williams, showed the influence of James Brown, with George Duke's soulful piano keeping pace. Olga Adderley contributed another vocal on her self-penned "Amani." *Down Beat* praised the album, but it proved to be an unsuccessful close to Cannonball's eight-year stay with Capitol.

20

AS AMBIENT AS ALL HELL

After completing a Newport Jazz Festival tour of Europe in October and November 1972, Cannonball Adderley began hosting a weekly talk show on Los Angeles' KNBC-TV. Titled *Ninety Minutes Starring Cannonball Adderley*, the program featured Cannonball conducting conversations with personalities in the music and entertainment fields. The initial program featured guest Nancy Wilson, who sang "The Masquerade Is Over" with Cannonball and an unidentified studio band. But between then and the end of the series, there were no further musical performances. Cannonball was a natural raconteur, blazing yet another trail as one of television's first black talk-show hosts. Unfortunately, the ratings did not reflect Cannonball's talents, and the show was canceled after thirteen weeks.

In March 1973 George Duke left the band to go out on his own. Duke's leanings toward electronic music had been stoked by his work with Frank Zappa's band, the Mothers of Invention, but by this time Cannonball Adderley was removing himself from the world of fusion and returning to his roots. He replaced Duke with the more traditional pianist Hal Galper, who was nevertheless schooled on electric piano, now an accepted instrument in jazz groups.

On the very day Galper came aboard, Cannonball Adderley left Capitol Records. Like David Axelrod, Cannonball had become disillusioned with the label's concentration on the bottom line ever since Alan Livingston's departure in 1968; Axelrod said that the company had lost its soul. John Levy arranged for Cannonball to sign a contract with Fantasy Records, which had acquired most of the catalog of the defunct Riverside label, where Cannonball had made his most acclaimed recordings. Cannonball also severed his partnership with John Levy and dissolved Junat Productions, retaining only their publishing company, Upam Music. Olga recalled that Cannonball complained that his band had been subsidizing all of the expenses needed to run Levy's management company and that they would have to "tighten their belt." David Axelrod said that Levy had taken a quarter of a million dollars from Cannonball's earnings without Cannonball's knowledge to help keep his management company afloat, and when Cannonball found out, he fired him. David Axelrod recalled:

> Cannon was going to dissolve the group. I don't know if anyone in the group knew it. Nat didn't even know it. Cannon was going to stop everything. A lot of people were just going out and hiring rhythm sections in whatever cities they were in. And Cannon knew everybody everywhere. He wouldn't have had any problems. He told me he was sick and tired of paying everybody a salary and paying their health [insurance]. They all had policies that Cannon was paying for. Had he lived, I'm convinced he would have cut the group loose.

On his first Fantasy album, Cannonball was reunited with his old friend Orrin Keepnews, whose involvement was a major reason Cannonball went with the label. The album was recorded on June 4, 1973, with Axelrod joining as coproducer. Keepnews liked Axelrod's practice of "bringing the club to the studio" and set up shop in Fantasy's Studio A in Berkeley, California, with an invited audience on hand. But Axelrod thought there were too many people in the studio: "It was so packed that the air conditioning couldn't serve the amount of people who were in the booth. I was sopping wet from it. I was so glad when that session was over, I can't explain it to you."

The album's title, *Inside Straight*, was meant to reflect the group's return to straight-ahead jazz and the salad days of "Mercy, Mercy, Mercy." The album's cover featured a comical photo of Cannonball sourly revealing the result of a chance draw, topping off an ace, deuce, three, and five of hearts with an eight of clubs. To complement the party atmosphere, Cannonball had Spencer Moore, his personal chef, cater the event (so that the band wasn't the only thing in the studio that was cooking). The Oakland disc jockey Bill Hall introduced the "sounds and soul" of the band. The result was, as Keepnews succinctly put it, "as ambient as all hell."

Keepnews wrote the liner notes, calling the Quintet "one of the happiest, hippest, most burning, and most swinging groups in the world today." The band didn't disappoint. They led off the session with the title track, co-written by Cannonball and Nat, which featured a pounding electric piano rhythm by Galper and a sound that returned to where the group had left off with Capitol before it took its detour into Fusionland. Nat Adderley revealed a new talent—the odd sound of him screaming into his cornet—but other than that it was like old times. Galper provided three compositions to the playlist, including the funky "Snakin' the Grass" and the sambalike groove of "Inner Journey." King Errisson was retained to augment the rhythm section (in effect making the group a sextet), his bongos giving the band a little rhythmic overdrive on the faster numbers.

On the group's second session for Fantasy, the Quintet backed their old friend Joe Williams in an album focusing on ballads and blues. George Duke was invited back to contribute funky electric keyboard licks, which helped revive Cannonball's recently dormant blues leanings. The return to their roots was made, according to comments made by Nat to *Cadence* magazine in 1992, "to maintain some prestige along with being straight ahead, because everybody else was getting a lot of money playing what I call rock and roll." Straight-ahead jazz was being squeezed out by rock on one side and fusion on the other. Where Cannonball had once explored musically adventurous terrain, he was now exploring thematic ideas. His next project would address the then trendy interest in astrology.

The album titled *Love, Sex, and the Zodiac*, was one of the few disasters in Cannonball Adderley's career. Although Chris Sheridan notes that the album may have been recorded in February 1974, some researchers have placed it as early as 1970, a leftover from a Junat session designated for release by Capitol. The album was an attempt to recreate Nat Adderley's *Soul Zodiac* LP from two years before, for the third time utilizing the Adderleys' friend Rick Holmes as narrator. This time the topic was mankind's needs for love and sex as represented by the signs of the astrological zodiac. Like a hip *Soul Train* guru, Holmes unctuously guided the listener through twelve musical and sexual fortune cookies, with the Adderley band again providing a variety of musical settings. Although the underlying music isn't bad, Holmes's advice concerning the integration of sex and love was hard to stomach, even in the Age of Aquarius, when "What's your sign?" became a popular pickup line at bars.

On Cannonball's next album, titled *Pyramid*, the Quintet returned to saner musical musings. This record featured more rock-oriented jazz as the former band member George Duke returned to add synthesizer sound effects and clavinet to the mix. The Quintet was also augmented by a couple of guest artists, pianist Jimmy Jones (on "Bess, Oh Where's My Bess?" from *Porgy and Bess*) and guitarist Phil Upchurch. The leadoff song, Hal Galper's "Phases," featured a lot of Duke's spacey swoops and special effects, while Nat's contribution was a funky tribute to the New Orleans trumpet player Melvin Lastie, who had died in December 1972 at the age of forty-two.

In late 1974 Cannonball Adderley embarked on what he believed would be his magnum opus. It would turn out to be his last.

21

WITH HIS HAMMER IN HIS HAND

Cannonball Adderley had been agonizing for four years over his idea of writing a musical based on the traditional American legend of John Henry, the steel-driving man. The first documentation of the legend was a 1909 article published in the *Journal of American Folklore*. The musical, which was to be titled *Big Man*, was to be unlike anything Cannonball had ever undertaken. He and Nat would write the music, while the lyrics would be written by the team of Diane Lampert and Peter Farrow.

John Henry was among the pantheon of American folk heroes that, along with Paul Bunyan, Davy Crockett, and Casey Jones, among others, constitute a legacy of songs and folk tales. The universality of its quintessentially American themes—pride, strength, diligence, the overcoming of overwhelming odds, and an indefatigable competitive spirit—inspired more recordings than any other native American ballad. It has crossed every musical boundary: black and white, rural and urban, acoustic and electric.

The story is based on a probably real person, an African American who helped construct tunnels for railroad tracks and who competed with a steam drill while working on the Big Bend Tunnel on the C & O Railroad line in Summers County, West Virginia, around 1870. As the story goes, the race between John Henry and the steam drill was meant to test the practicability of the machine. John Henry won the race, but only after driving himself literally to death after vowing to defeat the steam drill or "die with this hammer in my hand."

It has been speculated, owing to its structural similarity to other

Anglo-American ballads of the period and geographical region, that the original ballad may have been written by a white person. Because of its universal themes, the song entered both white and black tradition in the early years of the twentieth century. The first recording of the ballad wasn't made until 1924, when the white Georgia musician "Fiddlin'" John Carson recorded it on a twelve-inch 78-rpm disc for OKeh Records. It has since been recorded by countless artists, from white artists like Burl Ives, Tennessee Ernie Ford, and Hoyt Axton to black performers like Lead Belly, Big Bill Broonzy, and Harry Belafonte. Prior to Cannonball Adderley's epic production, lengthy versions of the John Henry tale were recorded by Josh White (a double LP for Elektra in 1955) and Johnny Cash (an eight-minute version for Columbia in 1962). It has been recorded in folk, bluegrass, blues, country, rock, pop, jazz, and sacred music traditions. John Henry's exploits have been heard everywhere, sung by everyone from chained Negro convicts in Southern prison farms to slick urban folkies on the 1960s television program *Hootenanny!*

The legend of John Henry continues to be as timely in the twenty-first century as it was when it was first being told at least a hundred years earlier. The struggle between technology and the misplaced manual worker certainly resonates in today's world, where computers and complicated machinery are making muscle and bone obsolete. Even the staple of the American workforce, the automobile assembly line, has become superfluous in the face of more efficient, cheaper ways of doing the same work.

Diane Lampert had written lyrics for a variety of musical genres and artists, most notably the Academy Award–nominated title song (co-written with Peter Schickele) from the 1972 science-fiction film *Silent Running*, sung on its soundtrack by Joan Baez. Lampert's co-lyricist, Peter Farrow, collaborated with her on the 1961 television musical *O'Halloran's Luck*, starring Art Carney and Barbara Cook. Farrow wrote an original story based on the legend called *Big Man* that was adapted for the stage by Paul Avila Mayer and George W. George. Lampert had been looking for a composer to write music for the show for some years before Jo Basile King introduced her to Cannonball Adderley. After the Adderley brothers were engaged to write the score, production was delayed for a number of reasons, one of them the breakup of David Axelrod's marriage.

Big Man was the most ambitious treatment of the John Henry legend ever attempted. The stage musical would be accompanied by a double-LP gatefold cast album, complete with libretto, that was recorded during several sessions in late 1974. Starring in the title role was the former Count Basie vocalist Joe Williams. His co-stars included the twenty-one-year-old Randy Crawford, in her recording debut, and the stage actor Robert Guillaume, whose credits included the road version of *Purlie* and the musical revue *Jacques Brel Is Alive and Well and Living in Paris*.

The Cannonball Adderley Quintet, consisting of Cannonball and Nat Adderley, pianist Jimmy Jones, bassist Walter Booker, and drummer Roy McCurdy, was augmented by a full orchestra and chorus, as well as percussionists Airto Moreira and King Errisson. There was very little jazz in the show; Cannonball's only noticeable appearance on the album did not come until the last of the four sides, his alto sax wailing during the climactic steam drill race.

The music was a mixed bag of '70s funk, spirituals, and even some primitive disco leanings, with a few attempts at Gershwinesque balladry ("Who Bend the Rainbow?"). There were also shadows of George and Ira Gershwin's *Porgy and Bess*, first performed almost forty years earlier, in the production, with its all-black cast, overtones of the struggles of African Americans, and the inclusion of spirituallike songs ("Next Year in Jerusalem," "If I Was Jehovah").

Cannonball and Nat worked on the songs between 1971 and 1972. In 1972 Cannonball, Olga, and George Duke came down to Capitol Studios in Hollywood on a rainy Saturday to cut demos. Cannonball sang all the men's parts, Olga sang the women's parts, and Duke played piano.

A revised version of George W. George's script from November 1973, marked "Final," nevertheless contains songs that were not included on the cast album, including an opening number ("On His Bones"), a work song ("Rouster's Chant"), and a song in which workers bet on who will win the race ("Ten on the Engine"). Although the show was uneven and mannered, it did have its stirring moments, such as the chain gang song "Hundred an' One Year/M'ria" and the driving dissonance of the orchestra during the steam drill race. But despite the years of hard work put in by the Adderleys, Lampert, and Farrow, the album, which Cannonball had thought would be the crowning achievement of his career, instead became a desultory footnote.

Cannonball would later say, "I didn't look for this project. *Big Man* was the most difficult album I've ever done. I agonized over it for four years." In an interview after Cannonball's death for the *Washington Star*, Diane Lampert said, "He went into hock for this album, his other recordings being charged off to this project. He cut down his bookings and threatened to quit the business and teach. He was really sicker than he let anyone know."

Like the rest of Cannonball's albums for Fantasy, *Big Man* was not a success. David Axelrod believes part of the fault lay in the label's inability to properly market his records:

> When he left Capitol, his popularity really went down. I think that if he had not gone to Fantasy, if he had gone to a different label, he'd be as well known as Coltrane. When he came to Capitol, he was as well known as Coltrane. Toward the end, he was planning on buying his way out of his contract with Fantasy. He was going to pay them to let him go. The last time I spoke with him, he looked at me and said, "David, they're killing me." What a horrible thing, because the very next thing I knew, I'm getting a phone call saying that he had this stroke.

Early in 1975 Hal Galper left the band. The acoustically minded Galper had not been comfortable playing electric piano, and when he had had enough, he gave his notice. With the help of some national education grants, he returned to New York, where he formed a trio that played small nightclubs. In declaring his independence from the world of electronics, Galper later told *Down Beat* that he did so with "pure joy": "I wheeled the electric piano down in its case, tossed it in (the Hudson River) and watched the bubbles come up."

George Duke returned to his previous position as Cannonball's keyboardist, bringing along his synthesizer to play a space-age version of "Dis Here" at a two-day session at Fantasy in February 1975. Also joining the band were Cannonball's classic rhythm section, consisting of his old friends Sam Jones on bass and Louis Hayes on drums. The album, titled *Phenix*, was completed in March and contained fusion-influenced remakes of some of the band's classic works, including "Sack o' Woe," "Work Song," "The Jive Samba," "74 Miles Away," and "Country Preacher."

Sometime during the winter of 1975 Cannonball was carrying his luggage through Chicago's O'Hare Airport when suddenly he discovered that he was having trouble walking. The moment passed and he went on, but, as Olga Adderley later discovered, he had most likely had a minor heart attack. The stress of *Big Man*, combined with an already dangerous physical condition aggravated by his excessive weight, poor eating habits, and diabetes, had made Cannonball a ticking time bomb. It was inevitable that sooner, rather than later, catastrophe would strike.

In early June the Quintet played at Playboy clubs in Phoenix and Los Angeles before flying to Anchorage, Alaska, where they put on yet another high school concert and workshop. They then traveled to Kansas City, where they appeared at the Kool Jazz Festival.

On June 24 and 25 Cannnonball participated in what would be his last recording session, completing five songs for Fantasy with drummer Jack DeJohnette and bassist Alphonso Johnson sitting in for Roy McCurdy and Walter Booker. Joining them was reedman Alvin Batiste, a friend whom Cannonball had enticed away from a teaching career in Louisiana. The Brazilian musicians Airto Moreira and Hermeto Pascoal arrived the next day to contribute a song Pascoal had written the night before, "Nascente," which means "of the rising moon." The song would be Cannonball's last recorded effort.

They were scheduled to finish the session after completing their next road tour, which began in Uniondale, New York, followed by a concert at the Milwaukee World Festival. Cannonball's final performance took place, fittingly, before the students of Stenson Junior High School in Milwaukee. After that, the band split up for some time off. Nat, Walter Booker, and their new regular pianist, Mike Wolff, all went home, while McCurdy remained with Cannonball to transport the equipment back to New York by car. They left Milwaukee on July 12. McCurdy remembered:

> We had done two performances of *Big Man* and were right in the midst of getting it off the ground. They were thinking of taking it to Off-Broadway is my understanding of it. We were also getting involved in a lot of college dates at that time.
>
> We had just finished playing in Milwaukee, doing the jazz fest there. And then the band was off, so the whole band went back to

their homes and Cannon and I decided to drive on to Gary, Indiana. We had a van with all the instruments in it and everything, and stopped in Chicago. He loved to eat so we got a lot of barbecue and we drove to Indiana and checked into the Roberts Motel.

That night, I went up to his room and he had all this barbecue on the table so we went up and ate some. The next morning, I went down and had breakfast and then went back to my room. Around noon, I got a call from Cannon and he said, "Hey, I'm goin' down to eat breakfast, why don't you come on down and join me." I told him, "Well, I just ate but I'll come down and have some coffee with you." He said okay, but when we got downstairs, the restaurant was closed. He was talking to one of the waitresses who was cleaning up down there, trying to get her to open the restaurant so he could get some food. He had this charm he tried to put on everybody, calling her "darlin'" and everything, but then he just started slapping his face. When he tried to speak, all he could say was "mm-mm." He had lost control of his left hand and was trying to hold it up. He was obviously having a stroke.

Some people who had been in the restaurant in the hotel said, "We have to get him to the hospital. It's only a few blocks away." So we put him in a car (we didn't call for an ambulance) and started driving to the hospital. On the way to the hospital, when we were about a block or two away from it, we got broadsided by another car in the middle of the street. Bam! So I got him out and carried him in my arms. Adrenaline. Another car came up and we put him in that car, with me holding him in my arms.

By that time, people had called from the hotel to the hospital to let them know we were on our way over there. When we got there, all these nurses and doctors were standing outside to get him when he came in. By that time, he was already paralyzed on one side. He was still conscious but he couldn't talk. I stayed with him upstairs and held his hand and stuff like that. He was in bed, just looking around. His eyes were real wide and once in a while, he'd kind of grunt.

The hospital called Olga in California. She flew out immediately and met McCurdy at the hospital:

By the time I got there, he was still conscious and still aware of his surroundings, but he couldn't talk. He wasn't paralyzed yet. But the next day, he became paralyzed and went into a coma. He was in a coma for nearly four weeks before he died. His parents came and stayed with him. I stayed in a motel there and the people were so kind to us. One of the things I remember was Pops Staples came to see him and wanted to know if we needed any money. It was so sweet of him to do that. Quincy Jones called every day we were in the hospital. He was a big friend. Julian had pretty good insurance but it wasn't the musician's union that helped, it was the Screen Actors Guild. Julian had done some work for them, so the money for his treatment wasn't a problem.

A specialist came to St. Mary Mercy Hospital to treat the stricken musician. After examining his patient, he told Nat to notify the entire family and to expect the worst. Nearly four weeks later, on August 8, 1975, Cannonball Adderley died. He was forty-six years old.

Nat was devastated. For twenty years the two brothers had worked side by side, playing, traveling, and recording together. Although the band was always billed in Cannonball's name, it really belonged to both of them. Cannonball had kept secret even from his brother the stroke that he had suffered in 1958 when he was with Miles Davis. Cannonball knew that his days were numbered and feared he would not live past forty; Nat never suspected a thing. David Axelrod, a close friend of Cannonball's, was not surprised when he heard of the stroke:

> I knew that he was a diabetic because one of the first things he ever showed me was how to give him a shot of insulin and where he kept it. It was in his attaché case. We always got adjoining rooms. Always. And the door between them was never locked. So one morning I got up and went in to have breakfast with him and saw him lying on the floor. I knew what it was, went over and got the syringe, gave him the shot, and he perked right up. I really cursed him out too, for not taking it. He hated needles. That's why he never became a junkie. If he wouldn't have hated needles, he would have become a junkie because he was always around guys who *were* junkies. But he never

messed with needles. I would always tell him two or three times a week to lose weight. He was so heavy, it was absurd. Far, far heavier than he should have been, especially being a diabetic.

Axelrod recalled that Olga carried Cannonball's cowboy hat on her lap all the way down from Gary to Southside Cemetery in Tallahassee, where Cannonball was laid to rest. Said Axelrod:

> He never should have been buried in Tallahassee. He hated Tallahassee. He should have been buried in L.A. He really loved L.A. But Olga couldn't fight off Nat and Cannon's parents. It was too much for her and she gave in. That's the reason Nat didn't want me to come to Gary. He said that nothing could be done but that I was going to be a pallbearer at the funeral. The funeral was incredible. All the state houses in Florida had the flags at half mast, like he was their favorite son. When he was a kid, he couldn't even go to the beach because they were segregated. Tallahassee was eighty percent black and they had all the blacks piled into a beach that was a quarter of a mile long. That's why Cannon never would have wanted it done there.
>
> Jesse Jackson did the eulogy and it was magnificent. He was at his height then. The pallbearers included four people who knew Cannon was he was young, and then there was Walter Booker and myself. He was very tight with Booker.

Engraved on Cannonball's tombstone are the words: "God smiles on certain individuals and they get the privilege to have certain beautiful artistic vibrations pass through them . . . Cannonball."

On August 18 a service was held at Florida A&M University, with Nancy Wilson and Jesse Jackson on hand. Memorials were also held in Los Angeles and New York. Florida declared September 15, 1975, "Cannonball Adderley Day." It would have been his forty-seventh birthday.

It would be some time before Nat was able to resume his career, but on October 31, at Orrin Keepnews's urging, he pulled himself together long enough to record one last song to complete the album Cannonball had started in June. Alvin Batiste returned to play saxophone, while

Nat brought in three special guests who had become especially fond of Cannonball: his nephew Nat Jr. on electric piano, Ron Carter on bass, and Jack DeJohnette on drums. Nat Jr. had written a song called "Lovers" that had already been designated for the album, but at the session the band recorded an extended version of it. Two months later a vocal by Flora Purim was added, with lyrics adapted from the book of Revelation in the New Testament. Two months after that additional parts were overdubbed by George Duke, Alphonso Johnson, and Airto Moreira.

The cover of the album featured the image of a medallion sculpted in Cannonball's honor by Legends in Our Time. It was commemorated on the first anniversary of his death, along with the world premiere of his musical, *Big Man*. On the reverse of the medal, one of Cannonball's own philosophical statements was inscribed, with a facsimile of Cannonball's signature. The inscription reads, "A Big Man is judged by others, not one's self."

22

BIG MAN

On July 2, 1976, the Newport Jazz Festival presented the world premiere of Cannonball Adderley's final opus, *Big Man*, at Carnegie Hall. Joe Williams reprised the role of John Henry that he played on the Fantasy album while Nat Adderley conducted his Basic Black and Blues Band. Other cast members included Denise Delapenha as Carolina, Paul Gleason as Bull Maree, and Dan Blakey as Jassawa. The cast presented the show in a concert version, holding scripts in one hand and microphones in the other. The sound quality was so poor that John S. Wilson, the *New York Times* critic, complained that the dialogue and much of the lyrics could not be understood. Yet he also noted that although Williams wore horn-rimmed glasses and read from a script, he cut an imposing figure as the steel-driving icon. Wilson praised Cannonball's work as "warmly melodic, full of evocative songs, lively dances, and moments of dramatic power" but concluded that *Big Man* deserved better than the slapdash treatment it had received. Tragically, this work, into which Cannonball Adderley had put so much effort, has rarely been performed.

Nat Adderley later told Chris Sheridan, "I couldn't face the bandstand and went into hiding for almost a year. Finally, that passed, but I never felt so lonely in all my life as when I played that first gig without him." In July 1976 Nat formed a quartet with John Stubblefield on tenor sax, Onaje Allen Gumbs on piano, and Buddy Williams on drums, performing a two-week gig at Hopper's nightclub in New York. He resumed his career and became a headliner not only in the United States but in Japan, Switzerland, Australia, and New Zealand.

Eventually diabetes struck Nat as well. In the 1990s his health started to decline, and in 1997 he had to have his right leg amputated. He died from complications from the disease on January 2, 2000, at the age of sixty-eight and was buried near his brother at Southside Cemetery.

Olga Adderley later married the folk singer and activist Len Chandler; the couple lives in Los Angeles.

Since his death, Cannonball Adderley has had a pronounced influence on several generations of saxophonists, becoming one of the most important musicians on his instrument since Charlie Parker. Although his musical *Big Man* proved to be a failure, Cannonball's many hits, including "Dis Here," "Work Song," "African Waltz," "Mercy, Mercy, Mercy," and others, have become staples in the jazz repertoire. The loss of Cannonball Adderley at such a young age robbed the jazz world not only of a profound musical voice, but of an extremely eloquent spokesman. It is no exaggeration to say that Adderley's efforts in promoting, teaching, and conducting clinics for students in countless high schools and colleges across the country probably did as much to stimulate interest and knowledge about jazz as anything any other musician had ever done. He was indeed a "Big Man."

Acknowledgments

Olga Adderley Chandler and Len Chandler
David Axelrod
Debborah Foreman
Laurie Goldstein and L'oro Music/Gopam Enterprises, Inc.
Quincy Jones
Roy McCurdy
Dan Morgenstern
Patty O'Connor
John Sellards
The Thousand Oaks Public Library

Sources

Interviews

Adderley, Cannonball
"Golden Tears," Newsweek, June 12, 1961.

George T. Simon, "A Group-Thinking Star," New York Herald Tribune, February 16, 1962.

Riverside Records press kit, summer 1962.

Interview with Jack Winter, KCFR, Denver, Colorado, January 31 and February 4, 1972; published in Coda 186 (1982).

Adderley, Nat
Riverside Records press kit, summer 1962.

"Cannon and I," *Metronome*, December 1960.

Interview by Monk Rowe and Dr. Michael Woods, May 29, 1995.

Axelrod, David
Telephone interviews with the author, March 11 and 14, 2012.

Chandler, Olga Adderley
Interviews with the author, Los Angeles, CA, November 15, 2011, and February 23, 2012.

Quincy Jones
Interview with the author, Los Angeles, CA, March 29, 2012.

Sources

Jones, Sam
Riverside Records press kit, summer 1962.

Lateef, Yusef
Riverside Records press kit, summer 1962.
Telephone interview with the author, February 25, 2012.

McCurdy, Roy
Interview with the author, Altadena, CA, February 29, 2012.
Interview with Monk Rowe, New York City, November 16, 1995.

Zawinul, Joe
Riverside Records press kit, summer 1962.

Bibliography

Baker, David. 1980. *The Jazz Style of Cannonball Adderley*. Miami:
    Studio 224.
Billboard
Charles, Ray, and David Ritz. 1978. *Brother Ray*. New York: Dial Press.
Davis, Miles, with Quincy Troupe. 1989. *Miles: The Autobiography*.
    New York: Touchstone.
Down Beat
Eggelletion, Andre Michael. 2010. "Nation Mourns the Loss of FAMU
    Marching 100 Founder Dr. William P. Foster." realdealtalk.com.
    August 28.
Gibbs, Terry, with Cary Ginell. 2003. *Good Vibes: A Life in Jazz*. Lanham,
    MD: Scarecrow Press.
Glasser, Brian. 2001. *In a Silent Way: A Portrait of Joe Zawinul*. London:
    Sanctuary.
Haskins, Jim. 1977. *The Cotton Club*. New York: Random House.
Hicock, Larry. 2002. *Castles Made of Sound: The Story of Gil Evans*.
    Cambridge, MA: Da Capo Press.
Jazz Review
Lydon, Michael. 1998. *Ray Charles: Man and Music*. New York: Routledge.
Metronome

Mingus, Charles, with Gene Santoro. 2000. *Myself When I Am Real: The Life and Music of Charles Mingus.* New York: Oxford University Press.

Nelson, Scott Reynolds. 2006. *Steel Drivin' Man: John Henry—The Untold Story of an American Legend.* New York: Oxford University Press.

Nisenson, Eric. 2000. *The Making of "Kind of Blue."* New York: St. Martin's Press.

Owens, Thomas. 1995. *Bebop: The Music and Its Players.* New York: Oxford University Press.

Ruppli, Michel, with assistance from Bob Porter. 1980. *The Savoy Label.* Westport, CT: Greenwood Press.

Segell, Michael. 2005. *The Devil's Horn: The Story of the Saxophone, From Noisy Novelty to King of Cool.* New York: Farrar, Straus & Giroux.

Sheridan, Chris. 2000. *Dis Here: A Bio-Discography of Julian "Cannonball" Adderley.* Westport: Greenwood Press.

Shipton, Alyn. 2010. *Hi-De-Ho: The Life of Cab Calloway.* New York: Oxford University Press.

Szwed, John. 2002. *So What: The Life of Miles Davis.* New York: Simon & Schuster.

Whitburn, Joel. 1985. *Top Pop Albums: 1955-1985.* Menomonee Falls: Record Research Inc.

Whitburn, Joel. 2000. *Top Pop Singles: 1955-1999.* Menomonee Falls: Record Research Inc.

Yanow, Scott. 2003. *Jazz on Record: The First Sixty Years.* San Francisco: Backbeat Books.

Discography

Cannonball Adderley's recording career consisted of recordings he made not only as a leader, but as a member of other groups as well. For the sake of expediency, we are including only a list of recordings issued under his name. These include original 33⅓ long-playing (LP) issues released in the United States during his lifetime. A fully comprehensive listing, including compact discs, 45-rpm singles, posthumous reissues, imports, and anthologies would be too lengthy to include here. Readers who are interested in examining Adderley's recording career in greater detail are encouraged to consult *Dis Here: A Bio-Discography of Julian "Cannonball" Adderley*, compiled by Chris Sheridan (Greenwood Press, 2000) or visit www.cannonball-adderley.com.

Unless otherwise stated, all dates are recording dates rather than release dates.

1955

Presenting Cannonball (Savoy MG-12018)
Julian "Cannonball" Adderley (EmArcy MG-36043)
Julian "Cannonball" Adderley and Strings (EmArcy MG-36063)

1956

In the Land of Hi-Fi with Julian "Cannonball" Adderley
  (EmArcy MG-36077)

1957

Sophisticated Swing (EmArcy MG-36110)

Cannonball Enroute (EmArcy MG-20616) (released in 1961)

1958

Cannonball's Sharpshooters (EmArcy MG-36135)

Somethin' Else (Blue Note LP-1595)

Portrait of Cannonball (Riverside RLP 12-269)

Jump for Joy (EmArcy MG-36146) (released in 1960)

Things Are Getting Better (with Milt Jackson) (Riverside RLP 12-286/1128)

1959

Cannonball Adderley Quintet in Chicago (Mercury SR-60134)

Cannonball Takes Charge (Riverside RLP 12-303/1148)

The Cannonball Adderley Quintet in San Francisco
  (Riverside RLP 12-311/1157)

1960

Them Dirty Blues (Riverside RLP 12-322/1170)

The Cannonball Adderley Quintet at the Lighthouse (Riverside RLP-344/9344)

Cannonball Adderley and the Poll-Winners (Riverside RLP 355/9355)

1961

African Waltz (Riverside RLP-377/9377)

The Cannonball Adderley Quintet Plus (Riverside RLP-388/9388)

Know What I Mean? (with Bill Evans) (Riverside RLP-433/9433)
  (released in 1962)

Nancy Wilson/Cannonball Adderley (Capitol T/ST-1657)

1962

A Child's Introduction to Jazz (Wonderland RLP 12-1435)

The Cannonball Adderley Sextet in New York (Riverside RLP 404/9444)

Cannonball in Europe (Riverside RM-499) (released in 1967)

Jazz Workshop Revisited (Riverside RLP-444/9444)

Cannonball's Bossa Nova (with the Bossa Rio Sextet of Brazil)
  (Riverside RLP-455/9555) (released in 1963)

1963

Nippon Soul (Riverside RLP-477/9477)

1964

Cannonball Adderley's "Fiddler on the Roof" (Capitol T/ST-2216) (released in 1965)

Live Session! Cannonball Adderley with the New Exciting Voice of Ernie Andrews! (Capitol T/ST-2284) (released in 1965)

Cannonball Adderley Live! (Capitol T/ST-2399) (released in 1965)

1965

Domination (Capitol T/ST-2203)

1966

Great Love Themes (Capitol T/ST-2531)

Mercy, Mercy, Mercy! Live at "The Club" (Capitol T/ST-2663) (released in 1967)

1967

Why Am I Treated So Bad! (Capitol T/ST-2617)

74 Miles Away/Walk Tall (Capitol T/ST-2822)

1968

Accent on Africa (Capitol T/ST-2987)

The Cannonball Adderley Quintet "In Person" (Capitol ST-162) (released in 1969)

1969

Country Preacher (Capitol SKAO-404)

1970

The Price You Got to Pay to Be Free (Capitol SWBB-636)

The Cannonball Adderley Quintet & Orchestra (Capitol ST-484)

1971

The Black Messiah (Capitol SWBO-846)

1972

The Happy People (Capitol SAAB-11121)
Music, You All (Capitol ST-11484)

1973

Inside Straight (Fantasy F-9435)

1974

Love, Sex, and the Zodiac (Fantasy F-9445)
Pyramid (Fantasy F-9455)

1975

Phenix (Fantasy F-79004)
Cannonball Adderley, "Big Man"—The Legend of John Henry (Fantasy F-79006)
Lovers . . . (Fantasy F-9505) (released in 1976)

Index

Index

Index